The Wit and Wisdom
of Tony Banks

The Wit and Wisdom of Tony Banks

*A Tribute to a
Parlimentary Character*

Edited by Iain Dale

Robson Books

First published in Great Britain in 1998 by Robson Books Ltd,
Bolsover House, 5-6 Clipstone Street, London W1P 8LE

British Library Cataloguing in Publication Data
A catalogue record for this book is available from the British Library

ISBN 1 86105 200 6

Typeset by Pitfold Design, Hindhead, Surrey.
Printed and bound in Great Britain by
St Edmundsbury Press Ltd, Bury St Edmunds, Suffolk

For John

Contents

Introduction   1

Mandy Wouldn't Like It   5
The Grantham Spam Hoarder   11
Councillor Major   19
Lower than Vermin?   25
Musings and Mutterings   47
The Reptiles of the Fourth Estate   55
The Banks Lifestyle   67
Points of Order   85
Parliament and Politics   97
Friends of Tony   111
The Beautiful Game   117
The Foetus and the Fingers   127
Dream Job   135
Maybe it's Because he's a Londoner   147

The Banks Career   155
Bibliography   157

Foreword

This is the third book of political quotations I have edited – and it has certainly been the most fun. The idea came from my previous two books on Margaret Thatcher and Tony Blair. Both books contain several quotes by Tony Banks, all of which were either funny or thought provoking. It soon became obvious that the chirpy Mr Banks deserved a book on his own.

I am grateful to my colleagues at Robson Books for all their hard work and advice and also to the numerous people who have given me sources for quotes and anecdotes which have been included in this book. In particular, thanks go to Paul Flynn MP, Tom Levitt MP, Tam Dalyell MP, Jean Corston MP, Maria Fyfe MP, Stephen Timms MP, Kevin Maguire of the *Daily Mirror*, Mark Seddon, Mari Jessell of LWT *Crosstalk* and to the indefatigable Andrew Roth of *Parliamentary Profiles* whose press cuttings files have proved indispensable.

I should make clear that this book has not in any way been endorsed by Tony Banks, nor has he provided me with any information himself. I hope he is not embarrassed by it because he shouldn't be. The book is summed up by its subtitle – a tribute to a parliamentary character. And these days, we need more of them.

Iain Dale
August 1998

Introduction

Matthew Parris once wrote that Tony Banks was fast becoming a national treasure. This book is a tribute to someone who speaks his mind no matter what the cost – even if it could be his job. Wit and repartee lie at the very heart of political debate, yet they are attributes which few present-day politicians possess. Banks has them in bundles.

Like many extroverts, Tony Banks is a surprisingly shy character, rarely allowing anyone to pierce the effervescent exterior. Hiding as he does behind the cheeky chappy façade, his adoring public sometimes fail to see that deep inside, there is actually quite a sensitive, bashful and modest personality. It is easy to fall for the stereotype Pearly King East End football nut without noticing the more cultured, suave and natural disposition that exists simultaneously.

Yes, Banksy likes his champagne. Would this shock the good burghers of West Ham and Newham? Possibly, but probably not. Unlike the rest of the country, East Enders remain oblivious to the present-day national trend of envying those who have made it. And Banks unquestionably has made it, albeit with a few hitches on the way.

As Minister for Sport at the Orwellian Department of

Culture, Media and Sport, Banks is in his element. Football is his first love, and doesn't he let everyone know it? Apart from possibly David Mellor and John Major, Tony Banks is probably Chelsea FC's most famous fan – not that his ministerial position prevents him from joining ordinary fans on the terraces. He much prefers that to accompanying Ken Bates to his seat in the directors' box – but then again, who wouldn't?

He is a keen collector of political memorabilia, having accumulated a vast (and quite valuable) collection of Charles James Fox items. Indeed, in July 1998 he put some of his collection up for auction at Sotheby's. At the time he said: 'I am selling to finance the purchase of other artefacts to develop my collection.' He views Michael Heseltine and Jeffrey Archer as his main rivals at political auctions. 'They are the sort who are not short of a few bob at auction.' Or anywhere else come to that.

A former researcher to Dame Judith Hart in the late 1970s, Tony Banks first came to national prominence during his period as Chairman of the ill-fated Greater London Council in the early 1980s. At the GLC he also had responsibility for arts policy, which gave him a platform for some unconventional views. In 1983 he was elected MP for Newham North West.

His first years in Parliament were characterised by inveterate opposition to the Conservative Government's plans to abolish the GLC, led by Ken Livingstone. Banks quickly gained a reputation in the Commons as a doughty campaigner and parliamentary wit. Speech after speech was made fighting the GLC Bill at all hours of the day and night. But the campaign was doomed to failure and Margaret Thatcher got her way. Banks has never forgiven her.

During the wilderness years in opposition he made several glorious attempts to be elected to the Shadow

Cabinet but they were doomed to failure. From 1986 he received 37, 42, 50, 62, 49, 41, 42, 41, 47 and 47 votes from his parliamentary colleagues. As his fellow MP Paul Flynn says in his book *Commons Knowledge: How to be a Backbencher,* 'Tony is a deeply serious man and has made original, perceptive speeches on animal welfare, drugs reform and Chartism. Sadly, so dazzling is his comedy, his serious persona is eclipsed into the shadows.'

In the late 1980s his reputation as the wittiest member of the House of Commons grew and his talents were rewarded by Labour leader Neil Kinnock who promoted him to a position on the Shadow front bench. He resigned from the front bench twice and most commentators believed his political future lay only in providing the country with acerbic asides and appearances on TV comedy programmes. He even won an award at the *Spectator's* political awards luncheon in the mid 1990s, but he refused to accept an award from a Tory magazine.

But Tony Blair surprised both Banks, and the general population, by calling him into his new Government in May 1997 as Minister for Sport. He felt as if he had died and gone to heaven.

For parliamentary sketch writers he has provided material for acres of column inches. He has been profiled more times than any other junior minister and is perhaps the highest-profile Minister for Sport since the memorable Denis Howell in the mid-1970s. He admits to being frustrated by his lack of power and despite a few early gaffes (or the floating of new ideas, as he would put it) has grown into the job and survived the first government reshuffle.

Long may he continue! It will be a sad day for British politics when characters like Tony Banks feel they must keep their thoughts to themselves for fear of misquotation or being stitched up.

Mandy Wouldn't Like it

Never one to conform, Tony Banks must be Peter Mandelson's worst nightmare come true. His political past shows he is hardly one of New Labour's most likely enthusiasts, yet he is one of the undoubted stars of the Labour Government. But he will never quite be able to escape his habit of saying something which causes the Labour spin doctors to splutter over their early morning Islington muesli . . .

'If my Hon. Friend wants a spliff, I will no doubt be able to supply him with one, but it will not be one that I have rolled myself.'

To Labour MP Nigel Spearing during a debate on drug misuse, 9 June 1995

'Perhaps the best idea would be to privatise the Church of England, to get in a regulator – OfGod or something like that – and a few consultants, and then start marketing the Lord who is suitable to the 21st century.'

On how to improve church congregations, Hansard, *11 December 1995*

'It will pay for next year's gin supply.'

On the increase in the Queen Mother's civil list allowance, Sunday Times, *18 May 1997*

'You are left wondering whether this is all part of a softening-up process.'

Responding to a speech by Kim Howells hinting that Labour should ditch its links with the unions, 16 September 1996

'If you're going to dump your fundamentals, dump your ideology and disown your history, you're going off into the desert without a map. Like Mark bloody Thatcher.'

On New Labour, The Independent, *1 October 1997*

'The trouble is that the Labour Party feels, to a certain extent, that it's got to control everything. If we make mistakes, or if there are differences of opinion, we have to bring them out more.'

New Statesman, *November 1997*

'We have connived. We have gone along with the Party shifting to the right in desperation to win an election.'

Interview with York University student magazine, quoted in The Times, *16 October 1997*

★

He and Peter Mandelson could hardly be described as ideological soul-mates. Indeed, at a fringe meeting at the 1997 Labour Party Conference Banks crept up behind him and silently made the sign of the devil. But there is a mutual respect. Mandelson knows Banks is a good link to left-wing backbenchers and Banks admires Mandelson's abilities as a political fixer.

'It's not fair to kick a man when he's down, but it's safer, isn't it?'

On Peter Mandelson's failure to be elected to the NEC, October 1997

'Do you ever get that scary, scary feeling that there's more than one Peter Mandelson? What are they really doing in Millbank Tower? They tell us it's a communications centre. Well, I reckon they're making Mandelsons up there and getting ready to store them in that Millennium Dome in Greenwich . . . When the clock strikes midnight on December 31, 1999, millions of Mandelsons will emerge from the Dome and civilisation as we know it will be at an end.'

At Tribune rally, 30 September 1997

'Peter is a sweet guy, you know. But I eat lots of garlic and I sleep with garlic flowers round my neck. So I'm safe . . . for the moment.'

The Guardian, 10 May 1998

'Some people have been saying Gordon [Brown] and Peter [Mandelson] don't get on. I asked Gordon about this and he said he didn't know because he hadn't spoken to Peter for 18 months.'

While introducing Gordon Brown to speak at Tribune's annual dinner, 25 May 1998

'He probably doesn't sleep at night at all.'

On Peter Mandelson, interview with Kirsty Young, Channel 5, 19 July 1998

'A kind of architectural penis envy.'

On the Millennium Dome

The Grantham Spam Hoarder

Margaret Thatcher represents everything Tony Banks hates in a Tory politician. He absolutely can't stand her. She abolished his beloved GLC, and in his eyes brought the nation to its knees over 18 years of absolute power. When Banks makes one of his witty asides about opposition politicians a semblance of affection is often to be detected. Not with the Grantham Spam Hoarder . . .

'She is happier getting in and out of tanks than in and out of.museums or theatre seats. She seems to derive more pleasure from admiring new missiles than great works of art. What else can we expect from an ex spam-hoarder from Grantham, presiding over the social and economic decline of the country.'

On Margaret Thatcher

'She is about as environmentally friendly as the bubonic plague. I would be happy to see Margaret Thatcher stuffed, mounted, put in a glass case and left in a museum. She believes that anybody who opposes her – whether the Opposition or one of her friends – must by definition be wrong. She is a natural autocrat surrounded by a bunch of sycophants, many of whom have betrayed everything in which they once claimed to believe. She is far more influenced by the example of Attila the Hun than Saint Francis of Assisi. She is a petty-minded xenophobe who struts around the world interfering and lecturing in an arrogant and high-handed manner.'

On Margaret Thatcher

★

'For the Prime Minister and her blue-rinsed hordes in the home counties, Ken Livingstone and his colleagues appear to represent the end of civilisation as they know it. It is clear that all that is nasty, mean-minded and authoritarian in the Prime Minister – and there is lots of it – comes to the surface at the very mention of the GLC.'

Hansard, *13 December 1983*

'We should appreciate that the Prime Minister is very much a creation of our time – a leader who can use the language of the populist while at the same time taking the country towards an increasingly authoritarian and centralised Government. That suits her nature, in which resides the second reason for the Government's current onslaught on local democracy. The Hon. Lady hates all opposition, whether it be inside or outside the Conservative Party.'

Hansard, *23 January 1984*

★

'I once saw a piece of graffiti on a wall in London – it might have been washed away by now – which said: "get rid of Thatcher before she gets rid of you" . A number of prominent Conservative Members have recently had experience of the sharp reality of that cautionary slogan, as the Tory Party gradually discards its higher minded and more principled leaders in favour of the parvenus who now dominate its higher councils.'

Hansard, *23 January 1984*

★

'The Hon. Lady says she bats for Britain. Apart from putting up the occasional dolly catch for her son Mark, all the signs are that her innings will end in a rather dramatic run-out for the British economy.'

Hansard, *24 February 1984*

'I do not deny that the Prime Minister is clever. But she is unimaginative, and it must be awful for the leader of a nation to be accused of lacking in imagination. I consider her to be nothing more than an unimaginative lower-middle-class Tory bigot.'

Hansard, *9 May 1984*

'She exterminates opposition within her own party as rapidly as she seeks to exterminate it from the Labour Party. We are dealing with an incipient Fascist who cannot tolerate any opposition in any circumstances.'

On Margaret Thatcher, Hansard, *9 May 1984*

'Is the Prime Minister [Margaret Thatcher] aware that her Government's policy towards local government now resembles "Son of the Titanic"? Before she sacks the Secretary of State for the Environment, that poor bumbling wreckage at the end of the front bench, will she bear in mind that he was only carrying out her instruction to abolish the Greater London Council, which was based on her own personal vindictiveness towards Ken Livingstone?'

Question to Margaret Thatcher, 5 July 1984

'We all know how expensive this Prime Minister's face is to the country.'

On Margaret Thatcher, Hansard, *3 December 1984*

'She is a half mad old bag lady. The Finchley whinger. She said the poll tax was the Government's flagship. Like a captain she went down with her flagship. Unfortunately for the Conservative Party she keeps bobbing up again. Her head keeps appearing above the waves.'

On Margaret Thatcher

'Did the Rt. Hon Gentleman [John Major] share my concern at the sight of Mrs Thatcher collapsing in a heap in Chile recently? May we have a debate next week on the way in which old age pensioners are forced to go abroad to earn a crust?'

At Prime Minister's Question Time after Margaret Thatcher collapsed during a speech in Chile, Independent on Sunday, *24 April 1994*

'Isn't it a disgrace the way the House has failed to honour the great achievements of Baroness Thatcher? We are deprived because there is no statue of her on the empty plinth in Members' Lobby along with Churchill, Attlee and Lloyd George. The citizens of Eastern Europe have enjoyed tearing down statues of Lenin and Marx after the fall of Communism. Let's erect a statue here to her, so that we can tear it down, now we have got rid of the old bag.'

Quoted by Paul Flynn MP in his book Commons Knowledge: How to be a Backbencher.

'The Prime Minister is an elected dictator. Hailsham said that about a Labour Prime Minister but it could more accurately have been said about Baroness Thatcher, who was an elected dictator. Her majority meant that she had no need to apologise to the country or the House. Had she wanted to add an eighth day to the week, she had the political majority to enable her to do so.'

House of Commons, 18 July 1995

'Is it not grotesquely unfair that some poor old cow, who has given a life of service to human beings in terms of delivering milk, ends up with a bolt through her head and is chucked into a fire? I know that one can think of a recent political equivalent, but the situation is not better for that.'

House of Commons, 1 April 1996

'She behaves with all the sensitivity of a sex-starved boa constrictor.'

On Margaret Thatcher, The Independent, *1 October 1997*

'When I think how Thatcher said nobody ever missed the GLC it makes me so angry. I mean, poor half-mad old cow, I shouldn't say anything but I want to be around to see us get our revenge.'

On Margaret Thatcher and the GLC, The Independent, *1 October 1997*

'I owe the Council a great deal. I'm determined to repay them. And that's why, when Thatcher, that provincial bigot, turns up and says: "They never did any good" over here, I just want to fill her face in.'

The Independent, *1 October 1997*

'I'm not really malicious. I have a list of people I loathe but it runs out once you've said Mrs Thatcher.'

The Guardian, *10 May 1998*

★

Kirsty Young: You sound very very New Labour. You sound more Thatcherite than Tony Blair almost . . .
Tony Banks: No, no, no. I would strongly object to the term Thatcherite being attached to my views.

Interview with Kirsty Young, Channel 5, 19 July 1998

★

Councillor Major

After seven years of parliamentary tirades against Margaret Thatcher Tony Banks was not quite sure how to play her successor. After all, he was almost a mate. John Major had served with Banks on Lambeth Council in the late 1960s. Gentle mockery replaced personal abuse.

'I have always found it a personal advantage to loathe my political opponents. It is not usually difficult, but the Prime Minister [John Major] is certainly not one of those. How could I? We both grew up in Brixton. We both like beans on toast. Where on this conjoined road of shared experiences did the Prime Minister go so badly wrong and become a Tory? I think that it was when he got turned down for the job of bus conductor. He had his heart set on punching tickets and helping little old ladies on and off the bus, but he was spurned. At that point he vowed hideous revenge on us all, but to be able to get it first he had to push a little old lady from Finchley off the bus. Having achieved that he has now turned his attention to the rest of us. Our fate is to be even more horrible than to be frogmarched out of Downing Street. We are to be buried alive under charters.'

The Guardian, *19 November 1991*

'I was delighted when I discussed it with him to find out that we occupied different ends of the pitch.'

On John Major's support for Chelsea FC, London Evening Standard, *26 October 1992*

'He was a fairly competent chairman of Housing [on Lambeth Council]. Every time he gets up now I keep thinking "What on earth is Councillor Major doing?" I can't believe he's here and sometimes I think he can't either.'

Independent on Sunday, *24 April 1994*

Tony Banks: Would it come as a surprise to the Prime Minister to learn that I am one of his admirers – indeed, I might be his only admirer? In that capacity, does he accept my great anger at the outrageous attack made on him by Margaret Thatcher, who, in her book, likens him to some sort of incompetent train-spotter? That is a disgraceful attack and I think that we all feel very strongly about it. Will the Prime Minister take this opportunity to damn all Mrs Thatcher's policies that have got him and his Government into the appalling mess in which they now find themselves.

John Major: The fraternity that exists between former Lambeth councillors perhaps does not entirely extend to the Hon. Gentleman. It is less of a surprise to hear that he may be an admirer of mine than a shock and a disappointment.

Prime Minister's Questions, Hansard, *23 May 1995*

★

'The Prime Minister [John Major] is, of course a fellow Chelsea supporter, although of less vintage than me. I was there for all Chelsea's championship year because it is the only one we have had. The Prime Minister has told me that he started to support Chelsea the following season. I was beginning to get rather worried because we have many similarities. We both come from Brixton, we were both on Lambeth Council and we are both Chelsea supporters and Surrey supporters. I took great consolation from finding that he stood at the opposite end of Stamford Bridge. Clearly, the divisions were evident even then.'

House of Commons, 8 June 1995

Tony Banks: Does the Prime Minister [John Major] recall his promise – indeed, his pledge, to construct a classless society in this country? If he really meant that, why is he so set against the proposal from my Right Hon. Friend the Leader of the Opposition [Tony Blair] to scrap the rights of hereditary dukes, marquesses, earls, viscounts and lords to speak and vote in the House of Lords? Could it just be that the boy from Brixton, whom I remember, has got a feeling to make himself into a nob after he leaves here? Does he really want to be remembered as the nob from Brixton?

John Major: I hope that the future Lord Banks will reconsider what he has said about that matter. My remarks about a classless society were about equality of opportunity, not about the grey uniformity the Hon. Gentleman would wish to see in this country.

House of Commons, 21 November 1996

★

'He revealed himself as a Thatcherite with a grin. He deserves to be called Tinkerbell as all he has done is tinker with the problems of the British economy.'

On John Major

★

'The idea that John Major could end up being voted Personality of the Year is so ludicrous as to beggar belief. It just indicates that the Labour Party has got an awful lot to learn when it comes to rigging polls. The Tories can always show us how it is done and get away with it.'

Daily Telegraph, *27 December 1996*

'Throughout the year, he stood like the boy on the burning deck of the *Titanic*, with his finger in the dyke, an apple on his head and his foot in his mouth.'

Awarding John Major the title of Survivor of the Year, The Guardian, *27 December 1996*

'He should have chosen something from the *Beggar's Opera* because there is a whole chorus on the London streets which could join in.'

On John Major's appearance on Desert Island Discs

'He is so unpopular, if he became a funeral director, people would stop dying.'

Courtesy of Kevin Maguire of the Daily Mirror

'Last time I heard about James Major and Emma Noble he was an assistant manager at Marks and Spencers and she was doing *The Price is Right*. Now they've apparently landed a £3 million float for a club. It's quite remarkable. With that sort of economic prowess his father should have made him Chancellor of the Exchequer.'

The Sundays, *Channel 4, 30 May 1998*

Lower than Vermin?

Aneurin Bevan once accused the Tories of being 'lower than vermin' – a maxim Tony Banks would surely approve of. Bevan was no mean orator himself and would surely have taken great delight at the way Banks assails the Conservative benches in the House of Commons.

Personal insults during a debate are the best way to force a parliamentary opponent to lose his stride. No one is better than Tony Banks at dishing out the insults. But they are hard to take personally.

'Tony Banks has a good way of not giving offence while making an amusing and often cutting comment.'

Tory MP Anthony Beaumont-Dark, the Observer, *22 October 1989*

★

'Perhaps to his own mortification, even Tories find it impossible to dislike him.'

Peter Oborne, London Evening Standard, *26 October 1992*

★

Tony likes to pick his prey carefully, and once chosen, they remain hooked, as right-winger Terry Dicks found out. Dicks prided himself on his philistinical approach to the arts and took every opportunity to speak out against subsidies to the opera and ballet. Cue Tony Banks . . .

'He is to the arts what "Bonecrusher" Smith is to lepidoptery. His views are philistine in the extreme, anachronistic and wholly unacceptable to any civilised body of thought.'

On Tory MP Terry Dicks

★

'He is an unreconstructed Member of Parliament. When he leaves the Chamber, he probably goes to vandalise a few paintings somewhere. He is to the arts what Vlad the Impaler was to origami. He gives us a laugh.'

On Terry Dicks

'Listening to him is like listening to Vlad the Impaler presenting *Blue Peter*. He is undoubtedly living proof that a pig's bladder on a stick can be elected as a Member of Parliament.'

On Terry Dicks

★

'The Hon. Gentleman [Terry Dicks] really is a most ungrateful wretch to speak in unkind terms about his former employer, the GLC.'

Hansard, *5 April 1984*

★

'He is a man whose contribution to the arts is about the same as Bluebeard's contribution to the institution of marriage.'

On Terry Dicks

★

'In arts debates he plays the court jester. He has a muscular approach. He claims that the ballet is something for poofters in leotards. That is the level of his contribution. He is to the arts what the *Sun* is to English literature, or what the A Team is to embroidery.'

On Terry Dicks

★

'The Terry Dicks tendency is behind us as well as in front of us.'

Pointing out that some Labour MPs also share Terry Dicks's views on the arts

The funny thing is, Terry Dicks never hit back. Maybe he was grateful for the publicity. Dicks lost his seat in May 1997 but Banks has now found a new target on the Tory benches, the Hon. Member for Staffordshire North, Michael Fabricant. Fabricant is best known for his luxuriant mane of Heseltinian hair . . .

'I congratulate the Hon. Member [Michael Fabricant] on becoming a Parliamentary Private Secretary, which is a humble if worthy job. It is the first greasy mark on the political pole, and we would all agree that few have greased more assiduously, or carried a ministerial lunchbox with more colour and verve than the Hon. Member for Mid Staffordshire. There is a certain guile about the Hon. Gentleman that neutralises his propensity to kiss the bottom of any passing figure of authority. He is visibly bursting with pride at becoming a ministerial gofer, which makes me rather sad. I do not see a Minister manqué sitting opposite but a poor, wretched youth congratulating himself on getting the last cabin boy's job on the *Titanic*.'

House of Commons, 24 July 1996

'Managing to put the camp back into campanology.'

On Tory MP Michael Fabricant

But being a good sport, Fabricant recognises talent when he sees it . . .

'I have to put up with Tony Banks blowing kisses to me across the Chamber and Dennis Skinner challenging me about my hair, but it doesn't bother me.'

Michael Fabricant, The Guardian, *7 October 1997*

★

Nicholas Soames, grandson of Winston Churchill and aide-de-camp of the Prince of Wales is another regular Banks target. Soames belongs to the 'couldn't give a toss' school of Tory MP. He really doesn't give a damn what is said about him and it shows.

'You could have an exhibition inside your own underpants.'

To corpulent Tory MP Nicholas Soames during questions on the Millennium Dome exhibition, House of Commons, 19 January 1998

★

'The amiable Crawley food mountain clearly likes his grub. At the dispatch box he could probably persuade MPs that arsenic is quite palatable if suitably chilled.'

On Nicholas Soames

★

'Who could loathe the Hon. Member for Crawley [Nicholas Soames] however much one might detest the colour of his socks on Friday or laugh discreetly at his Mr Toad wardrobe.'

Hansard, *27 April 1993*

'A cross between Sir John Falstaff and Bertie Wooster.'

On Nicholas Soames, Hansard, *27 April 1993*

Tory MPs themselves appear to regard it as quite a coup to be assailed by Tony Banks. In tennis terms you can almost see them lining up at the baseline to hit a soft ball over the net for Banks to volley back at them – aiming where it hurts . . .

Patrick Ground: Is that a shirt or a tattoo?
Tony Banks: At least I have a chest, which is more than the Hon. Gentleman has.

Hansard, 9 May 1984

'I do not suppose that members of the Soviet Union's armed forces are any more influenced by alcoholism than many Conservative Members appear to be.'

During a debate on discipline in the armed forces, Hansard, *3 July, 1984*

'That was hardly a question. It was more a statement of the Hon. Gentleman's [Christopher Chope] bigotry.'

On Tory MP Christopher Chope, Hansard, *27 March, 1984*

'I was not sure whether the Right Hon. Member for Guildford [David Howell] was speaking for or against the Bill, but perhaps he is rather like the man who sat on the fence waiting for the iron to enter his soul.'

Hansard, 11 April 1984

'I was waiting for the Hon. Member for Hendon South [John Marshall] to get round to the Schleswig-Holstein question. Next time he wishes to raise ten issues, perhaps he will bring out a little book and we can all buy it when it is duly remaindered.'

House of Commons, 22 May 1996

'On a point of order, Mr Speaker. Some of us are trying to listen. However, I believe that the Minister [William Waldegrave] is determined that we shall not hear him. He is mumbling and speaking too fast because he does not want us to hear what he is saying. I do not think he believes what he is saying.'

Hansard, 17 January 1984

'Why should they suffer?'

To Tory MP Robert Hughes who, complaining about the working hours of the House of Commons, said he was going to reintroduce himself to his family to remind them who he was, Financial Times, *5 July 1991*

'I say that if the Minister [Douglas Hogg] was standing in line waiting to die, he would fill his underpants, and probably has.'

On the BSE crisis, Hansard *12 March 1997*

'May I say, en passant, to the Minister [Iain Sproat] that I was very disappointed that he did not present the Coca-Cola Cup at Wembley and that the Secretary of State got the job? We all know how much she knows about football

– the Cabinet's answer to Alan Hansen. Then again, I suppose that life is a bit of a bucket of cold spit; the Minister does get the topless dancer tossing the caber.'

House of Commons, 1 April 1997

Ken Clarke is another Tory who, Banks likes to pillory, but you sense that deep down he quite likes him . . .

'Pot-bellied old soak.'

On Kenneth Clarke, Hansard, *21 June 1994*

'It was an amazing scene yesterday when the Chancellor of the Exchequer [Kenneth Clarke] was at the Dispatch Box. It was the political equivalent of Landseer's *The Stag at Bay.* I know that he is a rather portly stag, but rabid hounds were all around him – well, they were not all around him; they were all behind him.'

Hansard, *2 December 1996*

'In his usual arrogant and high-handed fashion, he dons his Thatcherite jackboots and stamps all over local opinion. He is like Hitler with a beer belly.'

On Kenneth Clarke

★

And believe it or not there are other Tories who Banks decides to tease rather than launch the full grenade at . . .

'The acceptable face of Tory extremism.'

On Sir George Young, Hansard, *24 February 1984*

★

'The Government's most proficient bullshitter.'

On Tory MP Steven Norris

★

'Scarcely capable of walking and chewing gum at the same time.'

On Lady Olga Maitland, Hansard, *31 January 1994*

★

'His contributions to debates are as if the House was not made up of Members of Parliament, but of delegates, all with their blue rinses and red necks applauding to the rafters, rather similar to when he makes one of his speeches to the Conservative Party Conference.'

On Michael Heseltine

★

'I have supported the lottery both by my actions in the House and by my activities in purchasing lottery tickets. I want to win, I desperately want to win because, apart from anything else, it would mean that I could escape from having my bottom bored into rigidity by having to listen to another interminable speech by the Hon. Member for the City of Chester [Gyles Brandreth]. I do not think I would have any difficulty in adjusting to being filthy rich. After all, enough Tories have managed it. I see no reason why I could not do the same. It would be pina coladas all round.'

House of Commons, 25 October 1995

'I regard him as the acceptable face of Conservative extremism.'

On Tory MP John Bowis, House of Commons, 12 July 1995

'He looks like Neville Chamberlain's PPS.'

On Tory MP Hugo Summerson

'It is marvellous how strong tea can produce so much wit.'

On Tory MP John Wilkinson, Hansard, 12 December 1984

'Even if he is announcing the most mundane point, he always makes it sound as if he is announcing the terms of the Treaty of Versailles or that the first Briton has landed on Mars.'

On his pet hate John Gummer, Financial Times, 5 July 1991

'Tarzan and the chimp.'

On Michael Heseltine and John Major, 19 October 1992

But there are some Tory politicians who Banks just loathes – and he can't hide it. In amongst the wit and insult there is some real anger . . .

'It is a great pity that the Secretary of State cannot find the time to stay with us for an hour. Perhaps he has nipped off to plug himself into his life support machine for a while.'

On Nicholas Ridley, Hansard, *13 November 1984*

★

'Vicious mill-owner.'

On Tory MP Dr Charles Goodson-Wickes, Hansard, *4 December 1996*

★

'When my Hon. Friend [Mark Fisher MP] becomes the new Minister responsible for the arts, I hope that he will go through the lists of appointees and not show any affection for Old Etonians merely because he is one of them. I hope that he will be cheerfully slitting throats. That is what we want in this place; we want a bit of red terror when the Labour Government come to power. I want Labour Ministers going through the lists of the great and good – weeding out the Tories and all the friends of the Tories.'

House of Commons, 25 February 1997

'He has not actually practised sycophancy, because he is a natural sycophant.'

On Tory MP Nicholas Bennett

'A fine example of a political thug.'

On Tory grandee Cranley Onslow

'Not the most lovable person. The news that he resigned gave me cause for concern. If he jumped from Number 11 Downing Street, there would now be a very large hole in the road.'

On Nigel Lawson

'Brutal, graceless and almost a complete waste of space.'

On Nicholas Ridley

'At one point Portillo was polishing his jackboots and planning the next advance. And the next thing is he shows up as a TV presenter. It is rather like Pol Pot joining the Teletubbies.'

Tribune *rally, October 1997 as reported in the* Daily Telegraph

'It was just a little bit of uncustomary bile on my part that led me to say those unkind, ruthless and altogether accurate things that I said about him.'

On Tory MP David Amess, Hansard, *3 April 1996*

'That's the best view.'

On wanting to see the back of Sir Andrew Lloyd Webber from Britain, following his comments about Labour's tax

'Arrogant, self-satisfied, smug and complacent individual [who composes] pretty forgettable chocolate box stuff.'

On Andrew Lloyd Webber, Daily Telegraph, *19 September 1997*

'That this House welcomes the undertaking given by the multi-millionaire Sir Andrew Lloyd Webber that he will quit Britain should Labour win the General Election; believes such a promise provides an extra incentive to vote Labour; and looks forward to Sir Andrew keeping his promise.'

Text of an Early Day Motion tabled by Tony Banks in the House of Commons, 1997

★

'You wally!'

To Tory MP Tony Marlow, Hansard, 22 May 1984

★

'Yankee lickspittle.'

On Tory Minister Tim Sainsbury

★

'So stupid and smug.'

On Tory MP Peter Bottomley

★

'He sees himself as a walking ballot box.'

On Environment Secretary Patrick Jenkin, Hansard, 10 May 1984

★

'May I urge a little humility on the Minister when he replies to questions? After all, he has an awful lot to be humble about . . .'

On embattled Agriculture Minister Douglas Hogg, House of Commons, 3 January 1997

'The thought of Edwina Currie coming at the public on ten different channels makes even the strongest man balk.'

On the delights of cable TV

★

'Many Labour Members would like to see the Hon. Member for Dover [David Shaw] strung up by his fleshy parts in the dungeon of the castle.'

House of Commons, 16 December 1996

★

'We all now realise that the Secretary of State [Patrick Jenkin] has a glorious future behind him.'

Hansard, *5 July 1984*

★

'Only someone like Michael Howard, who has had his sense of irony surgically removed, would fail to blush as he utters the things he does.'

The Guardian, *27 December 1998*

★

'I don't like being dictated to by a rich greengrocer who lives in Mexico and pays no taxes here. I don't mind Tories being defeated by the voters but not by a greengrocer from Mexico.'

On Sir James Goldsmith, quoted by Simon Hoggart in The Guardian, *May 1996*

'A rich greengrocer. I don't see why someone who's a Member of the European Parliament in France, who apparently lives in Mexico, who pays no tax in this country, can go out and start buying up the political process.'

On Sir James Goldsmith, Daily Telegraph, *12 June 1996*

'Britain still has the reputation of being the dirtiest nation in Europe. That must have something to do with the raw sewage contained in Nicholas Ridley's speeches.'

'If the Hon. Member for Ealing North [Harry Greenway] will sit still for a while and keep his mind open and his mouth shut, he may learn something to his advantage.'

Hansard, *25 November 1983*

'I disagree strongly with the Right Hon. Member for Chelmsford [Norman St John Stevas] (who is) perhaps the only ancient national monument that the Minister did not mention in his opening remarks.'

Hansard, *14 June 1984*

'I shall not give way to the chinless wonder just yet.'

To Tory MP Edward Leigh, Hansard, *13 December 1983*

★

'Is he aware that this morning he is amply earning his reputation as the Secretary of State for Political Cock Ups.'

About Patrick Jenkin, Hansard, *29 June 1984*

'I am trying to give Government Members food for thought so that the Hon. Member for Salisbury [Robert Key] can marshal his arguments better than he usually does.'

Hansard, *14 June 1984*

'He always strikes me as being like one of the Marx Brothers when he stands up to make a speech . . . the rather sad one who keeps running into things and never does anything quite right.'

On Richard Tracey MP, Hansard, *3 December 1984*

And what do Tories say about our Banksy?

'We all know our place when the Hon. Member for Newham North West is around.'

Virginia Bottomley, House of Commons, 16 April 1996

'The only trouble with the Hon. Gentleman's bid for a traditional form of service in the Church of England is that it would unfortunately disbar his ever being invited to take part as he represents the shouty-louty tendency in the Church of England's approach. I would be very happy to have the shouty-louty tendency alongside the happy-clappy tendency, but the Hon. Gentleman will have only traditional forms of service. By his own proscription, we shall alas be deprived of looking forward to his preachment in his local parish church, which we might enjoy.'

Michael Alison MP, House of Commons, 24 February 1997

'The Hon. Gentleman is full of bright ideas and I can think of nothing better than his arming himself with a barrow and parading up and down parish churches in the Newham district advertising his strong faith in the prospects and benefits of the Church of England.'

Tory MP Michael Alison, Hansard, *11 December 1995*

★

'You can see a Tony Banks joke coming from the other end of Victoria Street.'

Chris Patten

★

'He must have a large brain to hold so much ignorance.'

Anonymous Tory MP

★

'When I went to the Young Vic recently, I was not certain whether Tony Banks would appear on the stage or in the audience. He is a natural actor.'

Tory MP Tim Renton

★

And yet more examples of Tony Banks launching verbal tirades on helpless Tories. All together, now ahhhh . . .

'We are attempting to discuss the orders from this side against the barracking from the disciples of Onan on the Tory benches that we have come to expect . . . I am trying to take the matter seriously but I get the distinct impression that Conservative Members are not doing so.

I am also trying to be charitable so I conclude that their reasons for not taking it seriously are not totally disconnected from the intake of alcohol.'

Hansard, *3 July 1984*

'I am attempting to speak above the babble of malcontents on the Conservative benches.'

Hansard, *22 May 1984*

'I was referred to as a hooligan by a Conservative Member. Frankly, knowing the Hon. Member who used the expression, I felt that it was something of a compliment.'

Hansard, *6 June 1984*

'Parliamentary sheep who would cheerfully follow her over the edge of a cliff.'

On Margaret Thatcher's backbench supporters, Hansard, *3 December 1984*

'May I put in a bid for Cecil's plonker? One careful owner.'

During a debate on organ transplants, 5 February 1989

'Thin gruel, hard cheese and poached bullshit.'

Banks's suggested menu for Tory breakfasts with businessmen supporters, The Times, *8 October 1991*

'I am not averse to crucifying a few Tories to celebrate the millennium or, indeed, feeding them to the lions.'

House of Commons 18 November 1996

'I have just paid £350 for a crown [Hon. Members: "Ah!"]. That may be funny for Conservative Members. If any of them want some free dental service outside the Chamber afterwards I should be more than happy to give it to them.'

House of Commons, 18 March 1997

'There are times when I find it difficult to work out whether the Conservative Government is vicious or ignorant. I have come to the conclusion that it is both.'

'There is very little which is decent in this government of second-hand car salesmen, Arthur Daleys and low life generally – on second thoughts, I have probably been unfair to second-hand car salesmen.'

On the Conservative Government

'It was a tax which was drawn up by some half-wit in the Department of the Environment. A tax which was unfair, unloved and unclear – a good description of Margaret Thatcher's government.'

On the Poll Tax

'What Victorian values mean to Conservatives is that many of them would be quite happy to see little boys once again earning pennies by going up chimneys.'

'When Conservatives describe weapons of death and destruction they become positively orgasmic. Looking at them, those are probably the only orgasms they are likely to have. Margaret Thatcher used to tremble with excitement at the thought of being able to press the nuclear button.'

'May I say what an excellent job the Deputy Prime Minister [Michael Heseltine] is doing in standing in for the Prime Minister? To be fair, it is perhaps not the most intellectually challenging task that he has had to face. I thank him for his great courtesy when he came over to Newham in his capacity as one of the Millennium Commissioners. I know that he is considering my borough as a site for the Millennium Exhibition. I am sure that he will use the judgement of Solomon in coming to the right conclusion and ensuring that Newham is chosen. I am not one of those whingers who complains about the squillions that it has cost to set up his department. I am sure that the taxpayer gets great value for money, and I wish the Right Hon. Gentleman a very nice day.'

House of Commons, 6 November 1995

'It is the Tory Party equivalent of the Hitler Youth.'

On the Young Conservative movement

'We could debate the distribution of organ donor cards, which all Hon. Members should carry, because in the unhappy event that any of us should meet an untimely fate, our organs could be donated, saving the animals from having their organs taken from them – although in the case of Conservative Members, looking for their hearts could pose some problems.'

House of Commons, 16 January 1997

★

'Comparing the two speeches [of Tony Benn and Neil Hamilton] is like comparing Demosthenes with Alf Garnett.'

★

And the Liberal Democrats don't escape a tongue lashing either, although it is normally his custom to ignore them and hope they will go away . . .

'I am intrigued by the Hon. Gentleman's breakfast cereal speech – all snap, crackle and pop.'

To Paddy Ashdown, Hansard, *22 May 1984*

★

'Woolly-hatted, muesli-eating, Tory lick-spittles.'

On Liberal Democrats

★

'It's very foolish to criticise Paddy [Ashdown] because he can kill with his bare hands.'

Daily Telegraph, *10 May 1997*

Musings and Mutterings

'There was an occasion when I walked round the corner and was faced with an appalling dilemma of seeing a £1 coin embedded in a dog turd. I was left with a problem. There was a natural, primitive, capitalist, acquisitive instinct and a need for hygiene. As it happened, on that occasion, the hygiene won. But I managed to find a small boy who, for a crack of 50p, was prepared to retrieve the coin. He washed his hands in my house, and we put the money in the cancer box.'

During a debate on dog licensing, Hansard, *15 December 1987*

'We are all New Labour now.'

Evidence to the Select Committee on Culture, Media and Sport, Hansard, *14 May 1998*

★

'Bringing the leadership to its knees occasionally is a good way of keeping it on its toes.'

On the Tory leadership struggle in 1990

★

'I disagree with her description [Ann Cryer MP] of herself as "Old Labour". She may like to join us old Labour people; we describe ourselves as "Vintage Labour", which is slightly more in keeping with how we feel at the moment.

House of Commons, 23 July 1997

★

'Now I look back on it, that was the best month I've ever had. I suppose it's all downhill from here.'

On May 1997, the month Labour won the election, he was appointed Sports Minister and Chelsea won the FA Cup, quoted in Tribune, *15 August 1997*

★

'Does the Right Hon. Gentleman [Michael Alison MP] agree with ex-Archbishop Runcie that people want to go to church for traditional services? They do not want to be felt up by someone sitting next to them on the pew but go to have the hand of God laid on them; they go for a good quaff from the communion cup and a good hymn. Perhaps the Church Commissioners should follow the example of football and bring in a few Italian stars and a bit of razzmatazz. That might get a few more people going and putting money on the plate.'

House of Commons, 24 February 1997

'There are a lot of sad people.'

On being told that he had been voted Britain's third best looking MP by New Woman *magazine*

'I seem to represent some of the dirtiest constituents in the country, and what's more I say so in the local papers. That was the gist of my New Year's message to the good folk of Newham – that they were a pretty filthy bunch who should clean up their act.'

Hansard, 11 January 1996

'My mind is very open and so is my mouth – as you've probably gathered. Hopefully I can synchronise them.'

Daily Telegraph, 16 May 1997

★

'Soft porn.'

Description of women's tennis due to emphasis on 'knicker shots'

'More likely to be out nicking TVs than watching them.'

On children in his constituency, quoted in Private Eye, *16 February 1990*

'Britain is heading pell-mell towards the status of a banana monarchy but without the benefit of bananas.'

'For the benefit of those Hon. Members who think that I live in a concrete jungle I should point out that many cattle once wandered on Wanstead Flats, which is in my constituency, and it was a delight to see them. I have not seen them around recently, but I suppose that they have gone the way of all flesh.'

House of Commons, 13 November 1996

'There are people parking on double yellow lines who put on their hazard warning lights and think that they have dematerialised. It is time that the police stepped in and took more effective action, instead of zooming around London in large vans keeping their helmets dry.'

House of Commons, 10 February 1997

'In my mind, I have represented my country in every sport other than synchronised swimming.'

House of Commons , 7 June 1996

★

'Anyone who revealed the underwear secrets of the Hon. Member for Southwark and Bermondsey [Simon Hughes] deserves a great tribute from the nation. When he [Mark Thomas] revealed to a horrified nation the state of the Hon. Gentleman's underpants, he did something that we should all be pleased that he did. The underpants from hell is the only way in which I can describe them.'

Defending comedian Mark Thomas's satirical TV programme, Hansard, 3 April 1996

'If a Prime Minister needs political advice, he or she should not be Prime Minister.'

Hansard, *22 May 1984*

'I most certainly do not bother to read my speeches because I know what a load of rubbish they are before anybody hears them.'

'Make way, make way, I'm an MP.'

According to his fellow Labour MP Paul Flynn, this is what Tony Banks shouts in the division lobbies when he goes to vote

'How can you lose the re-run of D-Day?'

On the Government's plans for the 50th anniversary of D-Day, Independent on Sunday, *24 April 1994*

'I welcome the Minister to the Government dispatch box on the occasion of my latest and most enduring comeback.'

During his first question time as London spokesman, Hansard, *26 October 1992*

'I'm personally going to be pushing very hard for synchronised nose-picking. I think it has a great future, judging by the number of MPs who indulge in it.'

Quoted in the Observer, *1 February 1998*

'I'm afraid in the bottom-kissing world of politics in which we live, it's not what you say, it's who says it.'

The Independent, *1 October 1997*

'Socially Responsible Action Man.'

Suggesting renaming the Action Man doll

'It's getting quite fashionable to shag an MP these days.'

New Statesman, *February 1994*

'Has he requested anonymity?'

Upon being told the Chancellor had gained £325 million in tax revenues from the National Lottery

'I certainly didn't manage it until I was quite a bit older than most people. It really annoys me, even now, when I realise that so many of my most creative years were wasted in an unnecessary and unwanted celibacy.'

On sex

'If anyone is caught taking a picture of my bottom, he will get a sound thrashing.'

On being told of a photographer stalking round the Commons taking snaps for a Rear of the Year photo, The Times, *23 May 1996*

'They ain't gaffes. They are ideas.'

On his occasional outbursts, quoted in the Mail on Sunday, *March 1998*

★

'Very few Hon. Members of this House have ever understood local authority finance. There might have been three. Two of them are now dead, I think, and one of them is speaking.'

Hansard, *20 March 1984*

★

The Reptiles of the Fourth Estate

Tony Banks has a love-hate relationship with the media – they love him and he hates them. Well, most of the time. Let's face it, he wouldn't be who he is without the oxygen of publicity that the media provides him with. Unfortunately, his brushes with the media in recent years have led to a certain wariness entering his psyche. But who can blame him?

'There are plenty of journalist scum out there who'd like to get me. I'd be a nice scalp to get wouldn't I? But I'm not going to offer myself up to them on a plate. Fuck 'em.'

Independent on Sunday, *24 August 1997*

And so say all of us! Let's start with the affectionate tributes . . .

'The most amusing heavy leftist in sight.'

Edward Pearce, Daily Telegraph, *5 February 1987*

'All street cheek and quick wit – the nearest thing Westminster has to Jonathan Ross.'

Mark Lawson, The Independent, *9 February 1988*

'He has the persuasive powers of a market trader packing meat.'

Charles Nevin, Independent on Sunday, *24 April 1994*

'Tony Banks increasingly resembles the ex-dancer and celebrity Lionel Blair both physically and in terms of his act.'

David Aaronovitch, The Independent, *11 November 1995*

'Bill Cash should remember, never go on stage with children, animals or Tony Banks.'

Simon Hoggart describing a Banks mauling, The Guardian, *May 1996*

'The names Peter Stringfellow and Tony Banks rarely appear in the same sentence. After all, one's a sharp-dressed, silken-tongued smoothie, while the other owns a nightclub.'

Londoner's Diary, London Evening Standard, *21 May 1996*

'Tony Banks is metamorphosing into Captain Haddock, the permanently (and comically) enraged sidekick of Tintin the boy detective.'

David Aaronovitch, The Independent, *5 December 1996*

'Tony Banks is fast becoming a national treasure.'

Matthew Parris, Times *sketch, 19 January 1997*

'The nearest thing the House of Commons has to a music hall comedian.'

Sunday Times *Profile 18 May 1997*

'Cheerful Petticoat Lane crockery salesman.'

Guardian *Pass Notes, 19 May 1997*

★

Least Likely to Say: I strongly advise you not to call the Queen a silly old Trout, Prime Minister.
Most Likely to Say: Pass the bloody ball to Di Matteo you great tosser, or I'll have you both deported.

Guardian *Pass Notes, 19 May 1997*

'Without Tony Banks there could be some long silences in the saloon bar.'

Daily Telegraph, *20 August 1997*

★

'I don't think he can swim. He surely couldn't keep his mouth closed for long enough.'

Anonymous

★

'He ought to be a member of the Parole Board. He never lets anyone finish a sentence.'

Anonymous

★

'His pungent personal thesaurus is by and large unprintable. He is less of a chirpy chappy than a chirpy chippie – a male Madame Defarge who cackles as each new head drops into the basket.'

Petronella Wyatt, Sunday Express, *18 May 1998*

★

'Compact, eager and vole-like.'

David McKie, The Guardian

★

'An urchin Astaire.'

Mark Lawson, The Independent

★

'His performance as a cheeky chappie defies belief.'

Martin Ivens, Daily Telegraph

'Banks' lip, his street cred suits and streetwise insults bring the flavour of Newham to the corridors of Westminster.'

The Times

'I don't want this to sound wrong, Tony, but is the Government not *allowed* to sack you?'

They Think It's All Over *presenter Nick Hancock, November 1997*

'Eloquent is one word for him – lippy is another.'

Sue Mott, Daily Telegraph, *10 May 1997*

'Mandelson is going to have his work cut out with this one.'

Sue Mott, Daily Telegraph, *10 May 1997*

★

'Everyone knows that Banks was going to be the cabaret turn in Blair's government; first there was his record of Parliamentary brawling, and then there was the way in which he was blissfully unprepared for ministerdom – he hit the ground stumbling. On his first day, he bounded in half an hour late in jeans, having had to find out where the ministry was, and proceeded to lead the press upstairs to inspect his poky office. To fantasy footballers everywhere it was brilliant – as if the fans were bawling national anthems in the directors' box. To the civil servants used to stiff-collared subtlety, it was disconcerting.'

Article by Eric Bailey, Daily Telegraph, *August 18 1997*

'The Left's most effective comedian.'

Ian Aitken, The Guardian

★

'He is brave, original and outspoken – and an asset to British politics . . . Because Tony Banks is careless and tactless and sees the ridiculous side of life he has often said things that need saying. Banks may not be a wise man but he is clever – and has a kind heart. His clownishness hides a real concern for the poor and for people who have nobody to speak for them.'

Matthew Parris, The Sun, *6 October 1997*

★

'A total ape, baboon, buffoon, clown, harlequin, jackass, jester, joker, monkey, pantaloon, pickle-herring, scallywag, tomfool, half-wit, barmpot, headbanger, eejit numpty.'

Matthew Parris

★

'The leading bantam cock in Labour's awkward squad.'

★

'Both an accomplished sniper at the Government front bench and the funniest MP in the House.'

★

'Contrary to popular prejudice Mr Banks has his merits, not least of which is an inability to take himself or much else too seriously.'

Andrew Rawnsley, The Guardian

'I said to Tony Banks: "I think you're great." He is. He swears and everything!'

Sophie Dahl, Elle *magazine, October 1997*

'Heaven for Banks is an audience laughing at his jokes, a microphone recording them for posterity and a few diligent journalists writing them down, passing them on and generally reinforcing his reputation as a bit of a card.'

Patrick Collins, Mail on Sunday *5 April 1998*

It is astonishing how many journalists have already jumped on the 'Banks must be sacked' bandwagon since many of them make quite a good living out of following his every word.

'Snarling tsar of culture.'

Tabloid description of Banks during his year as chairman of the GLC

'That master of the wheedling and the unctuous – a left-wing fop who stoops lower to slide in the poniard than Uriah Heep did in deference to his betters – nothing too personal in that, I hope.'

Godfrey Barker, Daily Telegraph, *1984*

'Savage-hearted leftist whose jarring, exultant personality rings on the ears like a male tricoteuse.'

Charles Nevin, London Evening Standard, *10 November 1985*

'A vain, self-important little twerp.'

'Crossbencher,' Sunday Express, *15 November 1987*

'The suspicion lingers that behind a display of extravagant abuse lurks a fellow too cautious – or intellectually lazy – to show his own colours.'

The Independent, *12 November 1989*

'Banks merely operates in the toy department of life, the toothless sports ministry. The problem is that for a week or so some sections of the media have taken this preposterous figure half-seriously. Surely this cannot go on. Quotability is fine as long as there is a breadth of content.'

James Lawton, Sunday Express, *18 May 1997*

'Political career as the impudent voice of London. Ministerial experience but history of frankness verging on garrulousness.'

Independent on Sunday, *27 July 1997*

'No one will ever know how he got the job. By all accounts he is a lovely warm little cherub of the old Labour school, but one wonders how long he can sustain his job? So far his contribution has been totally useless.'

Ian Wooldridge, Daily Mail, *20 August 1997*

'Many regard him as a hugely refreshing blast of fresh political air and a great great wit. It is true that he is a dead ringer for a younger Reg Varney and would be odds-on for the lead in any parliamentary remake of *On the Buses* (with Peter Mandelson as Inspector Blakey . . .) . . . He is as amusing as non-specific urethritis and about half as appealing.'

Matthew Norman, London Evening Standard, *11 September 1997*

'I have no idea if Tony Banks is an able minister or not. He might well be. But it is impossible to tell beneath the thick layer of idiocy in which he has chosen to encrust himself.'

Kate Battersby, London Evening Standard, *6 October 1997*

'Mr Banks has barely been in government for eight months but he has already done enough to suggest that he is its least competent member . . . Mr Banks is an engaging character but, as he is the first to admit, he has got a very big mouth. He appears to lack any sense of tact or diplomacy and is virtually guaranteed to make a bad situation worse.'

Peter Oborne, Sunday Express, *18 January 1998*

'The back benches are to Tony Banks what music halls were to stand-up comics.'

John Cunningham, The Guardian, *10 May 1998*

And of course, the man himself is not without views on the abilities and frailties of Her Majesty's Fourth Estate . . .

'The average journalist was not at the front of the queue when brains were handed out.'

'I've stopped relaxing in the company of journalists and thinking aloud with journalists.'

Interview with Kirsty Young, Channel 5, 19 July 1998

'Semi-fascist comics.'

Describing The Sun, Daily Express *and* Daily Mail

'Listen mate, I'm gonna brick your bleedin' windows.'

To Rory McGrath on BBC TV's They Think It's All Over, *November 1997*

'Dead people can't sue.'

Talking about the tabloids being able to say what they like about Diana, Princess of Wales, Channel 4, The Sundays, *30 May 1998*

'Peter Hitchens is an objectionable lout and a bar-room bully.'

After refusing to appear on Any Questions *with him, 19 June 1998*

The Banks Lifestyle

It is common knowledge that Tony Banks is not averse to the good things in life – particularly a good glass of champagne. He says he is a vegetarian but one gets the impression it is because he thinks he ought to be, rather than because he wants to be.

'I do my best to be a vegetarian.'

★

'I have been a vegetarian for some years now, but unfortunately not long enough to have escaped the incubation period of mad cow disease in humans. So I am probably as potentially mad as anyone else in the Chamber.'

House of Commons, 3 April 1996

★

'I am a vegetarian. However I am nobody's turnip. I came to vegetarianism fairly late in my somewhat dissolute life; it has been a journey of discovery . . . I am however, no food fascist. If people wish to eat meat and run the risk of dying a horrible, lingering hormone-induced death after sprouting extra breasts and large amounts of hair, it is, of course, entirely up to them.'

Speech introducing a motion promoting vegetarianism, Hansard, *8 March 1995*

★

'I like sparkling wine. If I could afford it I would only drink champagne.'

Quoted in Sunday Times *18 May 1997*

★

'I like a drink myself and I am certainly not approaching this subject [health warnings on alcoholic drinks bottles] from a puritanical point of view. Indeed, for those who believe that alcohol is the devil's brew, I would remind them of the miracle of the wedding feast where Jesus Christ turned water into wine. Presumably he could have turned it into Rowntrees cocoa or Nestle's coffee, but for reasons that I would not dare to question he chose wine.'

Hansard, *8 June 1988*

'I got pretty pissed at university and I've never been pissed like that since. Over the years as an MP your tolerance builds up. I'm hardened. I'm no hair-shirt socialist. I like to relax and I like relaxing with a drink.'

The Observer, *8 December 1996*

He is also proud of his appearance, despite a few brushes with the fashion trade.

'Well, this is an Armani suit as a matter of fact; but I think me winning was more to do with me than my suits.'

On winning the Elle Most Stylish MP Award, Elle *magazine, October 1997*

'I don't think I'll ever get a six-pack stomach but that's the thing to aim for.'

Daily Star, *25 May 1998*

'I try to look a bit smart. It's as George Bernard Shaw said – if you're going to say unorthodox things, say them in unorthodox clothes.'

'Gold can look a bit vulgar.'

On his liking for silver jewellery

★

'I wish I had the courage to wear an earring.'

★

For someone who is generally viewed as extrovert, brash and outspoken, Tony Banks is really quite a sensitive soul deep down. Like many extroverts he is actually quite shy, allowing few into his private world. He wants to be loved, respected and revered, yet still appears to regard himself as a failure. Some of us beg to differ . . .

'I don't have a monstrous ego. I really don't. I have no ego at all. I find publicity unnerving because I don't regard myself as a politician – and neither do most of my colleagues.'

Total Football, *August 1997*

★

'Tony has his own personal demons that he wrestles with. He worries about whether what he does is worthwhile, and secretly fears that he is not good enough. His biggest problem is that he doesn't think he deserves to be happy and successful.'

American musician Aimee Mann, quoted in the Daily Telegraph

★

'I find that through humour one can actually make some very effective political points but I would not like to be

regarded as the Ben Elton of politics. What is important is
that people laugh with me not at me. As long as they are
laughing with you, then you are making your point well.'

Financial Times, *5 July 1991*

'I don't like pompous politicians. Unfortunately I tend to
spoil it by taking the piss, and there are times when I do
myself a disservice.'

The Guardian, *10 May 1998*

'I became a fairly minor casualty of the Gulf War. There
are times when the conscience becomes all-important. I
can defend things if I can convince myself. If I can't, how
the hell can I convince anyone else?'

On his resignation from the Shadow front bench, Financial Times,
5 July 1991

'No one can describe me as a brown noser.'

The Guardian, *10 May 1998*

'It's always nice to be a winner. I'm one of life's losers in
my opinion, so it's nice to get cheered for once.'

On winning the Elle *Most Stylish MP Award,* Elle *magazine, October 1997*

'Perhaps I'm just over-reasonable for politics.'

Interview with Kirsty Young, Channel 5, 19 July 1998

'My epitaph will be: He Was a Complete Tosser.'

'I'm one of those people that always thinks it's going to go pear shaped. I always look on the pessimistic side of life which means I'm rarely if ever disappointed. Putting it crudely, as I often do, I don't actually in the ultimate give a toss. I don't care whether I'm a Minister, I don't care whether I'm a Member of Parliament. I'll do my job to the best of my ability – that's all I can do. I am not ambitious. If I got a telephone call that said "Thank you Tone, we don't want you any more" I wouldn't care at all, any more than I was over-impressed when I was asked to be a minister. I was surprised yes, I'm not overawed, I'm not impressed, I don't think I'm in any way pompous because in the end I don't give a toss.'

Interview with Kirsty Young, Channel 5, 19 July 1998

'I'm very relaxed with myself.'

Interview with Kirsty Young, Channel 5, 19 July 1998

'Sometimes I'm appalled because I tend to throw myself into situations with more enthusiasm than judgement, and then I regret what happens afterwards, especially if I've said something spiteful or in poor taste. Good taste was never one of my qualifications.'

House *magazine, 10 April 1989*

'I find my life embarrassing.'

Daily Telegraph, *18 August 1997*

'I don't define myself by my country. I was born in Northern Ireland. I suppose I could call myself Irish. If I define myself in any way it would be European as I am a great believer in a united Europe. However, I would be much more likely to describe myself as an MP or Chelsea supporter. Part of this is that by virtue of being English or British, you do not tend to see yourself in terms of your nationality – the country has not been invaded since 1066. Nationalism more often arises as a unifying bond in times of national distress. I don't feel any need to define myself in this manner. I have the self-confidence to recognise that one should only be defined as an individual.'

★

Tony Banks has been at the forefront in parliamentary attempts to protect and improve the rights of animals. He has been a consultant to an animal welfare organisation and has spoken up many times against fox hunting, badger baiting and the export of live animals. He recently walked into a Westminster bookshop and asked for a large carrier bag. Into it he deposited an injured pigeon he had picked up off the pavement. Somehow it is difficult to imagine Peter Mandelson doing the same thing . . .

'I was once a keen angler, but I gave up the sport because I thought it was cruel.'

Hansard, *22 May 1984*

★

'Those who hunt foxes are no better in the final analysis than those perverts who bait badgers, course hares, hunt steers, stage dog fights and inflict mindless suffering on domestic pets and wildlife.'

Introducing a bill to ban fox hunting, Hansard, *27 April 1993*

'I ken we shall shortly welcome the day when we hear the last "tally-ho" and when John Peel will have to find something else to do with his horn in the morning.'

Closing remarks in the fox hunting debate, Hansard, *27 April 1993*

'If animals could vote, I am quite sure that I would have become Prime Minister by now.'

House of Commons, 13 November 1996

'Red-coated tossers on horseback.'

On huntsmen

★

'One knows from evidence of shark fishing in Japan that the shark is taken out of the water, its fins are cut off and then it is thrown back into the sea. A shark has to keep swimming in order to live and without its fins it cannot and it dies a horrible lingering death. Such exploitation makes me extraordinarily angry, because it shows no concern for other life forms. It is at that point that I lose all sympathy with and sentiment for human beings. I may go a little further than most people, but I just hope that I am around when that asteroid crashes into the earth and wipes out all life forms, as happened 65 million years ago. I would like to raise my glass of champagne to the asteroid as it comes in. Nature will then be able to start again and come up with a species that is somewhat better than human beings at living in harmony with the other creatures on this planet.'

House of Commons, 11 December 1996

'To ask the Lord President of the Council if he will take steps to exclude Turtle Soup and veal from restaurant menus within the Palace of Westminster.'

Written question, 11 January 1997

★

'John Peel's call might well have wakened the dead, but it has certainly stirred up the anti-hunting lobby and soon John Peel's modern followers will have to find something else to do with their horns in the morning.'

Daily Telegraph, *19 April 1997*

★

'He helps me to relax as he is slow and deliberate. I tend to be too hasty and aggressive.'

On his tortoise, Snotty

★

'They don't always use it. They've discovered that if they sit near the door, the alarm buzzer goes off and somebody has to come and let them in. It's no fun at 4.30am.'

On the nocturnal habits of his cats Buzz Lightyear and Felix, Daily Telegraph, *26 June 1997*

★

'I am a former piscatorial participant. I do not wish to sound immodest, but I was known in my day as a piscatorial artist – one of the finest.'

House of Commons, 27 June 1997 – he meant he used to go fishing!

★

Although a minister in the Department for Culture, Media and Sport, Tony Banks is thought only to care about his beloved football, yet his responsibilities include English Heritage and listed buildings – a part of his portfolio he takes very seriously.

'Cinema is essentially seen as entertainment rather than as an art form. That does not mean that something qualifies as an art form only if it bores the pants off everyone.'

Hansard, *19 November 1984*

I am an agnostic on lotteries. I would also like to be seriously rich, so I shall undoubtedly buy some tickets when they come my way. If I win, you will not see my bottom for dust.'

Hansard, *5 May 1994*

'The Hon. Member for Twickenham [Toby Jessel] spoke of the economic advantages of the arts. He has left the Chamber. I will forgive him for doing that, but I could forgive him almost anything having sat at a concert in Smith Square and having heard him play Mozart. It is fantastic to have such an ability and talent, which I did not associate with the Hon. Member for Twickenham. Given the way in which he jerks around all over the place, I thought it would be impossible for him to play Mozart, but he did so – and to concert performance standards. I found that it was a wonderful experience and I am deeply grateful to him for it. I could forgive him anything because of that ability to enrich my life and the lives of others through that beautiful music. He is a talented guy in artistic, if not political terms.'

Hansard, *5 May 1994*

'Art and politics go hand in hand.'

Daily Telegraph, *4 January 1997*

'In a world where countless millions are living in poverty, it is vulgar and obscene that so much significance should be attached to over-priced and grotesque flights of fancy for hanging on the limbs of the super-rich. In future, these clothing circuses should be treated with contempt.'

On high-priced designer clothing, The Times, *24 January 1997*

'When I ran the arts and recreation department at the Greater London Council I was referred to as the "snarling tsar of culture".'

House of Commons, 21 July 1997

'I'm sure it's a fine work of art, but here's me talking to people in this office about the end of tobacco sponsorship and I've got a picture of a bloody old geezer with a fag going.'

On a painting called The Red Flag *which hangs in his office,* Tribune, *August 1997*

'There is a lot of public support for dance sport, so damn those superior cynics who make snide comments and know nothing. They make me want to throw up.'

On ballroom dancing, The Times, *20 January 1998*

'Ballroom dancing has a level of civilisation about it. This makes it one of the more desirable sports.'

On ballroom dancing, January 1998

'The best career move is to die.'

On how to reinvigorate the career of a flagging singer, The Sundays, *Channel 4, 30 May 1998*

It is hard to imagine Tony Banks relaxing, let alone indulging in a bout of ballroom dancing. Here are a few random quotes about the Banks lifestyle and values . . .

'If you ask what I like to do, it is to stay at home and potter about.'

'I get angry quickly. I'm supposed to be the person looking after leisure, and my leisure time has gone. Reading, studying, watching television, spending time with friends – those things have gone out the window and I am deeply resentful of that. But that's the price to pay.'

Daily Telegraph, *August 18 1997*

'It was very permissive, in sexual terms, without any doubt at all. I must confess that my sex life was certainly more interesting then than perhaps it has been in recent years.'

Interview with York University student magazine, quoted in The Times, *16 October 1997*

'The permissive 1960s seem to have passed me by in all respects. I have made up for it in certain areas since then, but this [cannabis smoking] is not one of them.'

Hansard, *28 March 1994*

'I have never in my life taken or used illegal substances such as cannabis.'

March 1994

'Football; Parrots; Theatre.'

Tony Banks' interests in a political directory

'Banks Cock-up atoo (*Raucous squawkus*). A noisy, gregarious bird with tasteless habits. Notable left wing bias in flight. Too cocky by half but a good egg. Habitat: Chelsea.'

Description by Times *cartoonist Peter Brookes accompanying cartoon of Banks*

'I have a view on 'most everything, but then opinions are fairly cheap . . . I would like to have an awful lot more power.'

Hansard, *14 May 1998*

'There will be glitches in my transition from being a saloon bar sage to a world statesman.'

June 1997

'They've got it spot on. The link looks like it is going straight through my living room on the map. I'd laugh if it weren't my own house.'

On plans for the Channel Tunnel rail link to run directly under Maison Banks, 12 April 1993

'I have a personal concern about blight; the [Channel] tunnel goes immediately underneath my house. I am quite happy about that, but is there any compensation in this for me? My property, along with many others, has been blighted; its value has gone down. People do not want to buy a house over a tunnel.'

House of Commons, 1 November 1995

'Although the tunnel will go immediately under my house in Forest Gate, I cannot wait to sit in my front room and hear the rumble of the trains on their way to Stratford.'

House of Commons, 29 February 1996

★

'I always thought Mum ran everything. It was only when my old man died that I realised he'd been running the show. Mum even had to ask my wife how to cook.'

The Independent on Sunday, *24 August 1997*

★

'I loved my Dad to pieces. He loved a good argument and in many cases I know bloody well that he would take a contrary position in order to have an argument . . . I deeply resented him dying, particularly since the arsehole doctors didn't discover he was dying till it was too late.'

Daily Telegraph, *18 August 1997*

★

'I am a horny-handed son of toil who knows something about do-it-yourself.'

House of Commons, 9 February 1996

★

'I have a car at my disposal but it's actually easier for me to come in from the East End by public transport . . . it's most unlikely you'll see me walk out of here with a red box.'

Daily Telegraph, *10 May 1997*

★

'His lines are not bad . . . He has a good, natural poise. He's doing them better than some people who've been trying for years.'

Dennis Drew, ballroom dancing coach, on Banks's dancing abilities

'If I felt my old ticker couldn't take it any more I'd go like a shot.'

The Times, *3 February 1992*

'I prefer to be regarded as a passable politician rather than a lousy quiz-show panellist. I know my limitations.'

Sunday Times, *23 May 1993*

'I would take much pleasure in knowing that there are still bits of me circulating when I have gone to the upper chamber in the sky. Indeed, if bits of me were left for others to use, some unkind people might suggest that was the only decent thing I left to the world.'

During a debate on organ transplants, Hansard, *13 February 1984*

Points of Order

Speaking in the Chamber of the House of Commons can be a terrifying experience for any politician, no matter how experienced. Tony Banks admits to a bout of nerves every time he rises from the green leather benches.

'A sort of underpants-filling time.'

On asking a question in the House of Commons, The Independent, *16 March 1995*

★

Tony Banks feeds off the words of others but is quite happy to allow other politicians to show that they too can be as witty as Banks himself.

John Patten: The Hon. Member for Newham North West and I came dangerously close to becoming Hon. Friends because we agreed with each other for most of the debate. I pinched myself a lot. I regard him as a dangerous and wicked left-wing radical who is attacking the very fabric of society. I hope that helps him with his general management committee at his next constituency meeting.
Tony Banks: I am much obliged to the Minister.

Hansard, *6 November 1987*

★

Derek Spencer: 'On the town hall at Leicester, there is a monster with two heads . . .'
Tony Banks: 'It's Peter Bruinvels!'

★

Tony Banks: I wish to push the Secretary of State a little further. When can we expect an announcement? I have twice brought my sponge bag and twice I have returned home early. My wife clearly thinks that I am having an unsuccessful affair.
Nicholas Ridley: I really do not think that I can be held responsible for the disappointment to Mrs Banks.

Jack Straw: In a revealing slip of the tongue . . . the Prime Minister said that the Foreign Secretary had been 'instructed' by her – not, I suspect, for the first time or indeed for the last time – to get a certain deal and if he failed to do so . . .

Tony Banks: Off with his head!

Jack Straw: Yes, and it will no doubt happen at one of those 3am meetings at Number Ten. We are told that the Prime Minister and the Foreign Secretary do not sleep before 4am . . .

Tony Banks: And preferably not together.

★

Tony Banks: Is not the Chancellor of the Exchequer [Nigel Lawson] insulting the House by refusing to come here and make a statement on what is clearly a matter of grave significance for the economy? Not only does the Right Hon. Gentleman physically resemble Nero, but he is clearly adopting the same attitude. Will you confirm, Mr Speaker, that you have the power to order the fat bounder to be dragged here from the dinner table?

Mr Speaker: Order. First, I have not that power. Secondly, I dislike that expression, which I ask the Hon. Gentleman to withdraw.

Tony Banks: In that case, Mr Speaker, I shall say 'the corpulent bounder' .

Mr Speaker: That is almost as bad.

★

Tony Banks: The Hon. Member [Emma Nicholson] is skulking with the Minister's Parliamentary Private Secretary. Something very close and touching is going on and I wish I was part of it.

Emma Nicholson: We don't.

Tony Banks: Obviously the Hon. Lady is not into troilism.

That will take a while to sink in . . .

Emma Nicholson: The Hon. Member has recently tried his hand at male modelling. Although he has excellent suits and a good physique I would not give up the day job if I were him.

Edwina Currie: His physique is puny.

Tony Banks: The Hon. Lady has obviously been peeping because that is exactly what my wife says.

Broadcasting Bill Standing Committee, 1990

'On a point of order, Madam Speaker, will you explain a little bit more about how personal statements are arranged because one is beginning to get the feeling that they could happen every day? Perhaps we ought to exchange prayers for a confessional period. For example, would the ability to make a personal statement extend to Opposition Members? I have been sacked from Labour's front bench twice. Could I have made personal statements? In the unhappy event of my being sacked again, will you bear in mind that I have missed three previous opportunities? Could I take all three chances at once?'

Hansard, *10 June 1993*

★

'May we have a debate next week on facilities in the House of Commons? I have looked very carefully, but as far as I can see there are no condom machines in the House. I realise that their installation would come rather too late for some Conservative Members but it would probably be welcomed by the more circumspect among us. Alternatively we could seek some advice from Mrs Lorena Bobbitt, who has a very direct way of dealing with members?'

During Business Questions, 13 January 1994

'Was the story in the Sunday newspapers – that the Queen's head is too large for the Euro coin – true? If that is so, does the Prime Minister [John Major] intend to negotiate the size of the coin, or does he have more drastic measures in mind?'

Prime Minister's Question Time, 18 December 1995

'To ask the Chancellor of the Duchy of Lancaster if he will provide additional resources to enable the Faraday station [in Antarctica] to stockpile sufficient quantities of baked beans to last until the closure of the station?'

Hansard, *7 February 1995*

Tony Banks: I served my nation when at school by joining the Air Training Corps, where I became a sergeant, and I think the whole House can see the mess that it made of me. We do not need any lectures on the desirability of the cadet forces from a trio of white-feathered 'jobbies' in the form of the Prime Minister, the Deputy Prime Minister and the Secretary of State for Defence.

Tony Newton: I am left slightly open-mouthed by the Hon. Gentleman's description of his youth, which appears to bear little relationship to his adulthood.

Hansard, *23 January 1997*

Tony Banks: I have completely forgotten the second part of my Hon. Friend's [Ben Bradshaw] question. [Laughter.] These things happen; old men forget, as Duff Cooper once said.

Ben Bradshaw: After-school facilities.

Tony Banks: Yes, thank you. I am delighted that I am still hanging on in there, holed up in the DCMS with a 'Come in and get me copper' notice on the door . . .

Richard Spring: We are all crossing our fingers on the Minister's behalf.

On the day of Tony Blair's first Ministerial reshuffle, Hansard, *27 July 1998*

'Two words spring to mind in response to that answer. The first is "bull".'

House of Commons, 11 November 1996

★

We have already seen the results of Tony Banks's double act with Terry Dicks . . . But this has nothing on his spats with Shakespearean actor and former Labour MP Andrew Faulds. Faulds is an imposing six footer with a George V type beard and was well known as having a short fuse. Banks used to delight in winding him up, and Faulds was only too happy to let him. Parliament is a poorer place without him. It would have been marvellous to imagine what would have followed the Speaker's words: 'Questions to the Minister for Sport, Number 1, Mr Andrew Faulds . . .'

'Andrew Faulds has struck up a unique double act with the Newham left-winger Tony Banks who sits beside him. While Faulds is grand, bearded, commanding, as played by Orson Welles, Banks is compact, eager, vole-like: thereby achieving that juxtaposition of physical disparities which has distinguished all the great double acts from Laurel and Hardy to Steel and Owen.'

David McKie, The Guardian, *25 November 1986*

Andrew Faulds: We have had an excellent contribution from the Right Hon. Member for Chelmsford [Norman St John Stevas], whom I always thought was the best Minister with responsibility for the arts that we have ever had, and it is a pity that he lost the job . . .
Tony Banks: That's what he thought!

Hansard, *14 June 1984*

Andrew Faulds: On a point of order, Madam Speaker. You will be aware, as is the House, of the interminable interventions of the Hon. Member for Newham some-geographical-point-north-of-somewhere.
Tony Banks: Try North West.
Andrew Faulds: North West – thank you so much for that intervention. Would you not agree, Madam Speaker, that there is a sort of understanding in the House that, when one Hon. Member wishes to make reference to another, he gives that Hon. Member notice? It was drawn to my attention a few days ago that on an earlier occasion, the Hon. Member for Newham North West made reference to the discomfiture he suffered when I placed my buttocks beside him on this back bench.
David Winnick: Another scandal.

Andrew Faulds: Is there nothing sacred to this wanton boy? Is the House not aware that I have the most beautiful statuesque haunches, like carved Greek marble? Should the House not be aware that, when I place my buttocks beside the Hon. Gentleman, I get not a whimper of pain but a whinny of pleasure?

Hansard, 16 May 1994

★

Tony Banks: There is one point on which I will join hands with my Hon. Friend, the Member for Warley East . . .
Andrew Faulds: You are right for once.
Tony Banks: Just on this occasion, I think.
Andrew Faulds: What else are you offering?
Tony Banks: My Hon. Friend tempts me down paths of lasciviousness that I do not want to explore. Perhaps he could see me later.

House of Commons, 14 November 1996

★

Tony Banks: Will my Hon. Friend give way?
Andrew Faulds: If you must, yes.
Tony Banks: It is very sweet of you to give way to me, dear Friend. May I say to my very good Friend, whom I listen to carefully and from whom I have learnt a lot, that Martin Lee has made it clear that he intends to stay in Hong Kong after 30 June 1997. I suspect that he is running a damn sight more risks than my dear and Hon. Friend is running, even with his bad cold.
Andrew Faulds: I am sorry that my Hon. Friend had to comment on my cold, which somewhat spoils the organ that is my best achievement.

Tony Banks: That is not what I have been told.
Andrew Faulds: I think that matter had better be dropped.

House of Commons, 14 November 1996 (during a debate on Hong Kong)

Tony Banks: On a point of order, Madam Speaker. I know it said that Prime Minister's Question Time generates more heat than light, but am I having a heart attack, or could it be the light at the end of the tunnel? The luminosity in the Chamber seems to have been significantly increased, to the extent that I now realise how ugly Conservative Members are. Some of us like to skulk in the dark at the back of the Chamber . . .
Andrew Faulds: . . . May I say that I urge my Hon. Friend to lurk in dark corners more often, and not to assert his ugly profile so publicly and frequently?

House of Commons, 4 February 1997

★

Andrew Faulds: May I preface my question with an apology for turning up so late for foreign affairs questions? As you will recall, Madam Speaker, I have been an assiduous attender for many years. I have the best excuse in the world: I was entertaining to luncheon one of the most distinguished cultural figures in Britain, to whom the nation should be deeply grateful. I do not wish to publicise my name along with his name –
Tony Banks: It was Sir Les Patterson. [Laughter]
Andrew Faulds: I am a mite in the cultural world; this chap is a magnifico.

House of Commons, 12 March 1997

Andrew Faulds: The House will miss me. May I make as my last contribution, Madam Speaker, after 31 years of the most distinguished service, a valuable contribution to the proceedings of this august Chamber? When I first came here –
Tony Banks: Friends, Romans, Countrymen . . .
Andrew Faulds: Shut up, you silly boy!

House of Commons, 20 March 1997

★

'Loquacious windbag.'

Andrew Faulds MP

★

'Little whippet.'

Andrew Faulds MP

★

'Puerile comments from an inevitably loquacious colleague.'

Andrew Faulds on Banks's debating style

★

Parliament and Politics

Tony Banks, as the subtitle to this book says, is a consummate parliamentary character. He is proud to be an assiduous attender of debates and during his days as a backbencher regularly came top of the list of MPs who asked most written and oral questions. But one senses that the outdated traditions of parliamentary life are a source of frustration as well as providing him with a rich vein of material to ridicule.

'A legislative slum.'

On working conditions in the Palace of Westminster, Hansard,
20 July 1984

'This may be the only opportunity I ever get to speak at
the Opposition dispatch box so I have seized that
opportunity.'

Hansard, *21 December 1984*

'A Parliament of the politically undead.'

On the 1983-87 Parliament, Hansard, *5 May 1987*

'A legitimate protest.'

After he wore an African National Congress T-shirt in the Commons

★

'I don't believe we will ever be allowed to use Parliament
to achieve socialism. The obvious alternative is some sort
of violent overthrow of society, and that must remain a
possibility. We are a long way from revolution, and it
wouldn't give me any satisfaction, but I don't actually
believe the ruling classes would allow a socialist
government to change the whole basis and economic
structure through parliamentary means. It could well be
that a socialist government is elected and challenges the
system and a crisis follows which then might end in some
form of revolution.'

House *magazine, 10 April 1989*

'Fetchingly dressed.'

Comment on the attire of Speaker Bernard Weatherill, Financial Times, *5 July 1991*

★

'As a serious politician who wants to be where the power is, you have to follow it. That means moving.'

On his (as yet unfulfilled) plans to leave Westminster to become a Euro MP, Daily Telegraph, *13 April 1992*

★

'The book will tell aspiring MPs how to get away with doing no work whatsoever while at the same time appearing regularly on TV, going on every foreign trip available and attending all the best receptions.'

On his book Out of Order, Daily Mail, *20 January 1993*

★

' I have tried to keep in touch with the debate, but I have treated it somewhat like a buffet – dipping in and out while electioneering elsewhere.'

Hansard, *5 May 1994*

'Wouldn't this be a safer place to work if Members spent more time eating gooseberries rather than goosing?'

Hansard, *23 March 1995*

'Associating with zombies has always been something that I have been happy to do in this place.'

House of Commons, 14 June 1995

'Members of Parliament will spend more on the terrace this evening – so will I – than some individuals have to spend in a week. I am not claiming that I am impoverished – far from it. However, when I hear Members of Parliament going on about levels of benefit and how we need to ensure that they are appropriate, I realise that there is a great stench of hypocrisy, as ever, hanging around this place.'

House of Commons, 13 July 1995

'Since I was elected I have tabled 6,919 questions. If I had received £1,000 for each of these I'd have netted a cool £7 million, which would have meant that I could have faxed this speech from Mustique.'

On the cash for questions scandal, 13 July 1994

'All that has happened is that the fat cats have been put in charge of the creamery.'

On the lack of ordinary people of the a new committee to study directors' pay, House of Commons, 17 July 1995

'Let us have proportional representation; we might then achieve a balance in the House that is far more in keeping with the wishes of the people. Let us have fixed term Parliaments; let us abolish the House of Lords and the monarchy. Those are the ways to make the House more efficient.'

House of Commons, 18 July 1995

'If MPs are going to tighten the gun laws then I think Parliament should set an example by closing down this club in our midst and disposing of the weapons. We should be seen to be making the first sacrifice.'

Daily Telegraph, *19 March 1996*

'I would try and steer any children I had somewhere else. I'd say choose something more creative and intellectually fulfilling than being a Member of Parliament. The work is very tedious and time-consuming. There are much better jobs around, ones where you are doing something the public like – how about being a member of the Royal Family?'

London Evening Standard, *22 April 1996*

'Self-commendation is not a great thing in this place, which is full of people who think they ought to have been Prime Minister.'

House of Commons, 5 December 1996

'Words are cheap in the House. In some cases, they are almost useless.'

★

'I participate in the Lottery every week – in fact twice a week now. I would very much like to win. As I have said, I would fax from Mustique or wherever I happened to be my application for the Chiltern Hundreds when I won. I would not even bother to turn up.'

House of Commons, 25 February 1997

In his early days in the House of Commons Tony Banks was regarded by most observers as a fiery, left-wing radical. Despite the advent of New Labour he has hardly shed that image. His views on the monarchy are certainly Old Labour. He is an interventionist who believes it is the Government's responsibility to intervene in the economy to bring about a redistribution of wealth.

'I am unmoved by talk of the need to crack down on fraud, not because I am in favour of fraud, but because I am far more concerned about people who do not receive benefits to which they are entitled.'

House of Commons, debate on social security, 13 July 1995

'I do not want to be controversial, but rail privatisation is total lunacy.'

House of Commons, 7 February 1996

'It really is amazing to see the way middle-class people are so quick and willing to look after their own pet project, before looking around to see where the money is being raised in the Lottery. What we are seeing is the Lottery being used as a way of taxing the poorest areas and transferring the money into areas like central London.'

On the Arts Council's decision to give money to the Royal Opera House.

'Corrupt political systems inevitably produce corrupt economic systems. Honest business – if that is not an oxymoron – cannot long survive with a crooked Government. It is just possible for crooked business to try to survive under an honest Government, but if that Government are honest they will, of course, move rapidly to deal with crooked businessmen.'

House of Commons 14 November 1996

'This House calls for the establishment of a Royal Commission to review the prohibition of the use of cannabis and to examine alternative options for the control of the drug within the law; notes that millions of British citizens use cannabis for recreational and therapeutic purposes and that notwithstanding the enormous resources devoted by law-enforcement agencies its popularity and availability continues to increase throughout all parts of the UK and across all sections of society; also notes the growing body of evidence which testifies to the medical and therapeutic properties of cannabis and its relative safety compared with other legalised drugs; and believes that the prosecution of thousands of otherwise law-abiding citizens every year is both hypocritical and an affront to individual civil and human rights and that these resources are better spent on improving drug education, health and welfare programmes.'

Early Day Motion tabled by Tony Banks on 15 December 1993. It was supported by 21 MPs including Ken Livingstone, Simon Hughes, David Steel and Alex Salmond

His views on his fellow MPs can hardly be expected to win him many new friends . . .

'A pile of old doos.'

On the appearance of fellow MPs, Men's Health *magazine, October 1997*

'I look at my colleagues about my age and think, "My God, I look better than them because they probably look like shit anyway."'

Interview in Men's Health *magazine, October 1997*

'Nothing concentrates the minds of politicians more than impending political death.'

House of Commons, 14 June 1995

'I never usually intervene in Scottish debates because I am not someone who wants to end his life rather abruptly.'

House of Commons, 18 October 1995

'The only thing you can be certain about in politics is that you can't be certain about anything.'

BBC TV, 10 April 1992, the day after Labour's fourth consecutive election defeat

'Do you think ex-Ministers can get counselling? I'll get my head rubbed by a faith healer . . .'

The Sundays, *Channel 4, 30 May 1998*

'I can assure my Hon. Friend the Member for Kirkcaldy [Dr Lewis Moonie], the spokesman for the Opposition, that I will be supporting him in the lobby – I am nothing if not fodder.'

House of Commons, 25 October 1995

'Ferries encourage people to drink a large amount of alcohol while they make the trip. Getting as many bevvies down as possible is part of the fun. Many people taking part in an evacuation will therefore be inebriated, making it even more difficult. Perhaps the ferries should be dry.'

During a debate on ferry safety, House of Commons, 21 February 1996

'My speeches vary in content and pitch, and in the general level of boredom, hysteria, humour, intelligence, or whatever, so at least I can say that I vary the pace somewhat.'

Hansard, *21 January 1987*

If he wants to make a serious point he rarely flinches from using graphic language which goes against all the traditions of gracious speech-making. But he does it to drive a point home. If it makes people squirm, so much the better, as they will remember the point he seeks to make . . .

'The people who died [from BSE] in Scotland were not scared to death: they were poisoned. In his statement, the Minister [Douglas Hogg] mentioned excluding dirty animals. It is almost impossible to exclude faecal contamination from slaughterhouses, because the animals are standing in queues waiting to die. They can smell death, and when that happens, they urinate and defecate. If he was standing in a line waiting to die, he would fill his underpants as well – and probably has. The Minister must realise that meat-eating is bad for people's health. The people of this country should turn to vegetarianism before they turn as mad as the Minister.'

House of Commons, 12 March 1997

★

And if he gets too grand, there is always someone who is only too happy to bring him back down to earth . . .

'Clear those plates away, will you.'

House of Commons waitress who mistook Banks for a waiter due to his stylish waiter-like waistcoat!, Sunday Express, *12 July 1998*

★

Banks for Foreign Secretary. Now there's a thought! Diplomacy and Banks are two words that rarely appear in the same sentence. He is to diplomacy what Alf Garnett is to race relations. But at heart he's quite an internationalist, being a fervent believer in a single European state with a single currency and parliament. That doesn't stop him being rude about the Germans though . . .

'Could we have a debate on this country's relations with Germany? It is bad enough that the Germans get down to the beach first and rubbish our beef, but they have been pinching our balls.'

On Helmut Halle's attempt to keep the ball with which England won the World Cup, Hansard, 25 April 1996

'Our main competitors in Europe are the Germans and, without wishing to sound ungracious, I think on this occasion we have undoubtedly got our towels down at the swimming pool before our competitors.'

Evidence to the Select Committee on Culture, Media and Sport on England's 2006 World Cup bid, Hansard, *14 May 1998*

★

'I find it offensive to see the Japanese flag flying over County Hall, to be honest. Not that I have anything against the Japanese, except when they buy up County Hall and kill whales.'

Independent on Sunday, *24 April 1994*

★

'Those American, British and French pilots who have been risking their lives realise that they are facing weaponry that was provided by their own countries.'

February 1991

★

'President Bush would not know a principle if it were stuck on the end of an Exocet and smashed straight through his head.'

Hansard, *12 February 1991, during the debate on the Gulf War*

'I look forward to a socialist United States of Europe.'

June 1990

'I want a United States of Europe, with our own independent foreign and defence policies. Of course, it must be a democratic federal Europe.'

December 1991

'I want a United States of Europe because that is the most exciting prospect we have. I want a European government and a European president, and I want them to be based in a European Parliament.'

House of Commons, 12 December 1996

★

Friends of Tony

'Just before David Mellor resigned after his relationship with Antonia de Sancha had been revealed, Tony was musing over questions to ask him as Secretary of State for National Heritage. He finally came up with the following: "Was the Secretary of State the first person wearing a Chelsea strip to score twice in one night? Did the Secretary of State change ends at half time?"'

Courtesy of Jean Corston MP

'My first meeting with Tony was in his days at the defunct GLC. It was at the height of the war between Maggie's Westminster and Ken's County Hall. The papers had picked up on the 'loony' spending policy of the council. Tony, not unaware of this, would sit on the terrace of County Hall within sight and sound of the then ratepayers and, clutching a half lager, call out in glee: "It's all on the rates you know!" The abolition of the GLC failed to curb his ways. It was a habit he subsequently took with him to the House of Commons – substituting rates for taxes. Not hugely funny, but a taste of the man's irreverence.

Courtesy of Richard Bestic, Sky News

★

'Tony led for the Government in the Committee Stage of the National Lottery Bill. It was a good-humoured debate over several days, and we heard a number of contributions. Bernie Grant talked about how Lottery money could help Tottenham and Nigel Waterson gave an exposition of how Lottery money had been used in his constituency to relocate a whole lighthouse. In a moment of confusion, I interrupted Nigel "from a sedentary position": "What, to Tottenham?" There was much mirth and chuckling at this. Even the *Hansard* reporters saw the joke and they obviously thought it was very witty. How do I know this? Because the official report attributed my remark to Tony Banks!'

Courtesy of Tom Levitt MP

'Some years ago there was a debate about allowing women navy personnel to have jobs that required their being aboard ship at sea with male colleagues. One backbench Tory, of the Colonel Blimp school, objected, saying "We'll have women in the Guards next!" Tony quipped back, "Well, they'll be safe there, won't they?"'

Courtesy of Maria Fyfe MP

★

'Tony Banks got away with a cheeky question at a question time on foreign affairs. He stood and was not called on fifteen questions. He was greatly agitated about the threat of Norway to re-start whaling. Previously he caught the attention of the Nordics by suggesting that Norwegians should eat one another as an alternative to whale meat. He stood and was not called after mentally rehearsing tortuous links about questions on Panama, Sudan and Israel. Finally, the Speaker relented and called him. How was Tony going to link his plea with a question that asked "What action does the Government intend to take to increase the imports of bananas from the Windward Isles?" We held our breath. "Madam Speaker," he explained, "the people of Norway are going bananas about whales." Speaker Boothroyd was so amused that she let him get away with it.'

Anecdote from Paul Flynn MP

★

'Tony has been the star turn at the *Tribune* rally each year at Labour's conference for as long as anyone can remember. But the 1997 *Tribune* rally has to be the most memorable. Lapsing momentarily from the swashbuckling, laser-witted, tub-thumping style for which he is justifiably renowned, Tony suddenly adopted grammarless, humourless, New Labour-speak. The hall fell silent. Then like an East European bus queue who realise that the nightmare has passed, the crowd roared with laughter. Tony hadn't been got at after all. He was still one of them.'

Mark Seddon, editor of Tribune

'Because he lightens my day. He is the wittiest man in the Commons – I sit in front of him and it is most enjoyable. He is bright and also extremely determined and tough. He is a very clever parliamentarian and a good friend.'

Greville Janner on why Tony Banks is his favourite parliamentarian, The Observer, *22 October 1989*

'Having a reputation as a comedian has hurt old Banksy and it's hurt me.'

Ken Livingstone, Sunday Telegraph, *19 October 1997*

'The quickest heckling gun in the west.'

Austin Mitchell MP

'Sometimes his asides can distract from the serious business. If given the choice between saying something serious or making a joke, he will always opt to make a joke.'

Labour backbencher, quoted in the Financial Times, *5 July 1991*

'With every passing gaffe, his hold on ministerial office becomes increasingly tenuous.'

Labour spin doctor, 1 October 1997

The Beautiful Game

There is one job Tony Banks would have liked more than being Minister for Sport – playing centre forward for his beloved Chelsea. He loves football and uses it as a way to unwind and let off steam (as if he needed an excuse!).

'I have been an avid Chelsea supporter for more than 40 years. During that long period, we have not been spoilt with success. If one adds to that my membership of the Labour Party, I suppose that one can see that life appears to have dealt me something of a bum hand, but, in politics as in football, it is best to travel optimistically.'

House of Commons, 8 June 1995

'I would rather die than go to Arsenal.'

Hansard, 5 May 1994

'May I say to the Secretary of State [Virginia Bottomley] that there is nothing more artistic than a 40 yard pinpoint pass from Ruud Gullit or a pirouette from Gianfranco Zola on the football field? It is little wonder that football has been described as the working class ballet.'

House of Commons, 3 February 1997

'I was coached by Jimmy Hill when I was at school, which is probably why I can talk a better game than I can play these days.'

House of Commons, June 27 1997

★

'I couldn't possibly emulate the feats of one D. Mellor. Since the great days of Jimmy Greaves, it's the only time anyone's managed to score five times in a Chelsea shirt. The question we were all asking, of course, is did they change ends at half time?'

Total Football, *August 1997*

'There is a lot of similarity between football and ballroom dancing when they are both done well.'

The Times, *20 January 1998*

'For a Chelsea fan who has never had a formal dance lesson, Tony Banks MP is a natural-born mover.'

Ruth Gledhill, The Times, *January 1998*

'As lovely as a balletic pirouette.'

On the qualities of a good football pass, The Times, *20 January 1998*

★

Even before he became Sports Minister he held controversial views about the future of the national game – and even in government he has not been shy about airing them . . .

'We should ban the carrying of Union or national flags that are adulterated with the names of clubs or towns. These days the Union flag so often has the name of a club or the name of a town across it. The flag is supposed to be a unifying and not a divisive symbol.'

House of Commons, 8 June 1995

'We should cease the practice of playing national anthems before football matches.'

House of Commons, 8 June 1995

'Football is Thatcherism. If any area of leisure is calling out for some sort of regulation, it's got to be football. The one question is, how do we do it?'

Daily Telegraph, *2 October 1996*

'The 2006 World Cup should be held in South Africa . . . the claim by the African Nation [is] superior to that of any European country.'

Text of a Commons motion tabled by Tony Banks in December 1996

'There might be an argument for saying that if a player plays in this country for a League team then he can play for the country as well. The right to play would become not one of birth, but of residence. Instead of sitting there thinking "Well done, Zola" as he puts our international side down, wouldn't it be better if you thought "Hey Zola, you're over here and we're paying your wages, why not play for England?" My role is to be challenging and controversial and to act as a catalyst. Let's start thinking the unthinkable and see what happens.'

Daily Telegraph, *15 May 1997*

'Everyone thought it was a load of bollocks, fair enough - you're entitled to your opinion and I'm entitled to mine.'

On his suggestion that Gianfranco Zola should be entitled to play for England, Total Football, *August 1997*

'If football fans laid off the lager and were a little more Gaugin than Gazza, that might assist us enormously.'

House of Commons, 21 July 1997

'Some players are appalling role models and we don't expect the football authorities to be slack in the way they deal with them. Players can't have it all ways. They want the adulation and the hefty salaries, but they have to remember that they have responsibilities.'

Daily Telegraph, *31 July 1997*

'If I upset any of the fans or any of the players, then I apologise. Given the press coverage before the game the reaction was fairly understandable, but I didn't enjoy it and I still feel a little bit sore that what I said was taken completely out of context.'

On his hostile reception at Wembley having said that England were not good enough to win the World Cup, The Guardian, *12 September 1997*

'Itching for a fight.'

On the Italian Police at the England v Italy game, London Evening Standard, *13 October 1997*

★

'I am surprised at the number of footballers I see having a drag. Surely that can't be good for them as athletes?'

The Observer, *28 May 1998*

★

'I am the English Sports Minister. Our English fans have been very vociferous on this matter. I am listening very carefully to what our fans are saying and setting an example here.'

On his decision not to join any ministerial jollies to the World Cup Finals, The Guardian, *1 June 1998*

'I'm not happy about it, but I'll stand by what I said. When England or Scotland get to the final the Prime Minister will probably go but I won't be there.'

London Evening Standard, *4 June 1998*

★

It has to be said that Tony Banks is not universally admired in the world of football, but no one can deny he' s a true fan . . .

'No disrespect to anyone in the Royal Box, because I understand the Prime Minister will be in there, but since it's Chelsea playing and I'm a very demonstrative supporter, it would seem most inappropriate if I was leaping up and down hugging members of the Royal Family, or calling out that the referee's a wanker. Not to mention the fact that I shall be wearing my very large blue and white top hat.'

On why he wouldn't be sitting in the Royal Box at the 1997 FA Cup Final, Daily Telegraph, *10 May 1997*

★

'With Tony Banks in charge of sport, well quite frankly anything can happen.'

West Ham United fanzine editor Gary Firmager on Banks's call for terracing to be reinstated in football grounds, Over Land & Sea, *15 October 1997*

★

'The Newham Nutcase'.

Monty Burns, West Ham United Fanzine Over Land & Sea, *15 October 1997*

'You must be joking. Nothing would stop me going to the Cup Final unless I was dead. And if I was dead I'd want my ashes taken there.'

Asked if he would attend an EU Council of Ministers meeting if it clashed with the FA Cup Final, The Independent, *6 May 1997*

★

'It would have been nice if you would have been with me when I turned on the six foot fucking six bloke who called me a nigger lover in Bruges. And I was suddenly on my own when I told him what to do.'

Total Football, *August 1997*

'What do you do if you're a Tottenham fan? It's a bit much to have to start bashing up a Hewlett Packard computer!'

In response to a suggestion that in order to influence football clubs, fans should take on the club sponsors by, for example, pouring a can of Coke down the drain in front of TV cameras

★

'I'm not going to stop supporting my club because there might be an element of racist arseholes in the place. I'm not going to be forced out of my club because of that. I'm going to pitch in there and I'm going to support those who are doing their best to drive them out as well.'

Total Football, *August 1997*

'This man might be a fan but obviously he hasn't been briefed about the football world. On certain subjects it's better to think before you speak.'

Italian national soccer coach Cesare Maldini, Daily Telegraph, *15 May 1997*

'Ken [Bates], having done a lot of the hard work and slog, probably feels that Matthew, because the fans took him to their hearts as one of the lads kind of thing, received credit that Ken felt ought to go to him.' What I always say to Ken is "relax". Look around you and it's obvious that Ken Bates is the driving force in what has happened at Chelsea. Matthew played a significant role financially and psychologically at a crucial moment, but the real achievement is Ken Bates's.'

The Guardian, *17 October 1997*

★

'When God gave him [Paul Gascoigne] this enormous footballing ability, he took the brain out to equal things up . . . he's a great player, but likely to do the sort of thing that throws the whole team. I'll never forget that tackle in the Cup Final. Here's a guy that crippled himself trying to cripple someone else.'

Daily Telegraph, *25 May 1997*

★

'When I first heard about this new drug Viagra, I thought it was a new player Chelsea had just signed.'

The Sundays, *Channel 4, 30 May 1998*

★

'I'm fed up with seeing Tony Banks walking around in his Chelsea scarf. All I do is remind him which of our teams is higher in the League. That keeps him quiet.'

Arsenal supporter Chris Smith MP, quoted in the Sunday Express, *2 November 1997*

★

'I just paid £1,250 for next season's ticket at Stamford Bridge, "£1,250, yes, sir", and, Ms Ward, you may well look askance, but it is a drug and I cannot do anything about it.'

To Claire Ward MP, evidence to the Select Committee on Culture, Media and Sport, Hansard, *14 May 1998*

★

'They either don't know the history of the World Cup or someone has made une grande boo-boo.'

On the French World Cup Organisers, who omitted England from a list of previous winners, quoted in the London Evening Standard, *17 April 1998*

★

The Foetus and the Fingers

On the day Peter Mandelson failed in his bid to be elected to Labour's National Executive Committee, the Blair spin doctors were hard at work trying to find something to deflect political journalists away from the Mandelson story. Tony Banks was the fall guy. At a Tribune rally, where the audience expects the speeches to be both extreme and amusing, Mr Banks made a series of gags at the expense of senior figures in both main parties and brought the house down. Even the journalists laughed. Within twelve hours Labour's spin doctors had succeeded in persuading journalists that Banks had just gone one quip too far. And the journalists fell for it . . .

'To make things worse, they [The Tories] have elected a foetus as leader. I bet a lot of them wish they had not voted against abortion now.'

30 September 1997

★

'Filthy and offensive. This is one of the nastiest and wholly unjustifiable comments I have heard in 33 years in politics.'

Teddy Taylor MP, 1 October 1997

★

'Quite unworthy of a man who wishes to be taken seriously.'

Professor Scarisbrick, LIFE

★

'Sack this Clown.'

Daily Mirror *headline, 30 September 1997*

★

'This was a tasteless remark, uttered off the cuff, which I acknowledge caused offence and for which I fully apologise.'

30 September, 1997

★

'What a Banker.'

Daily Star *Headline, 2 October 1997*

'The Gaffe-r's Back in Town.'

Daily Star *headline, 3 October 1997*

★

'It was an unfortunate remark. He has made a very full apology for it. Let the matter rest there.'

Tony Blair, 2 October 1997

★

'He's a great guy with a great future.'

Tony Blair responding to journalists' questions about Banks's 'foetus' jibe against William Hague

★

'Personally I am grateful to Mr Banks. I shall never be able to look at Mr Hague again without thinking of a foetus.'

Melanie McDonagh, London Evening Standard, *2 October 1997*

★

'I know the difference between Tony Banks and a foetus. At least a foetus eventually grows up.'

Andrew Boff, Representative at the Conservative Party Conference, October 1997

★

'If people don't like the way I do things, stuff 'em.'

The Observer, *5 October 1997*

★

'I don't really need this grief, but I'm not going to be intimidated or harassed out of it by certain poisonous elements in the media. I know some people are gunning for me, and have been ever since I was appointed, but I believe people in sport know I love this job and that I am working hard for them. I'm not looking for a glittering career in politics. Tony Blair gave me this job with a phone call and he could take it away with a phone call, but I'm not stepping down. I see no reason to.'

The Observer, *5 October 1997*

'The Banks jibe about William Hague was in the worst of bad taste – but it was funny as Tony usually is. His trouble is that he cannot remember whether he is being Tony the Lad in a public house or a Minister of the Crown.'

Norman Tebbit, Mail on Sunday, *5 October 1997*

'At the end of the day Tony Banks will be fired not for a joke in bad taste but one in very good taste about Tony Blair's bosom pal, the oleaginous spin doctor Peter Mandelson.'

Norman Tebbit, Mail on Sunday, *5 October 1997*

'Was Tony Banks really in the mire, or did his foetus farrago conveniently wipe Mr Mandelson's National Executive sadness from short-term memory?'

Peter Preston, The Guardian, *13 October 1997*

'You might say that, I couldn't possibly comment.'

On suggestions that Labour spin doctors manufactured the row over Banks's foetus jibe in order to divert attention away from other problems.

Only a few months earlier Tony Banks had caused a minor row when he appeared to cross his fingers while taking the oath at the Opening of Parliament after the General Election. Again, his enemies pounced gleefully . . .

'I can uncross my fingers now.'

To House of Commons Clerk having crossed his fingers while taking the Royal Oath, 13 May 1997

'No insult or slur was intended by Tony Banks. The Minister was merely crossing his fingers for himself. Ten days ago he was a backbencher. He is now a Minister with responsibilities and duties.'

Downing Street spokesman, 13 May 1997

'I pick up pennies in the street. I am a very superstitious person. I'm always crossing my fingers. I was crossing my fingers, hoping to keep my job. It's such a wonderful job – like winning the Lottery, that I can't believe my luck.'

Daily Telegraph, *14 May 1997*

Is he demonstrating that the monarchy is so abhorrent to him that he cannot bear to swear an oath?'

Tory MP Iain Duncan-Smith, 14 May 1997

★

'Finger-crossing Republican Tony Banks should have read fellow Labour MP Paul Flynn's book *Commons Knowledge*'.

It warns MPs never to forget the TV cameras are on, even when taking the oath. Banks had less excuse than most for his slip – he wrote the book's introduction.'

Sunday Express *Diary, 18 May 1997*

Dream Job

Even before he was appointed to the job, it was clear that being Minister for Sport would be a dream post for Tony Banks, but one he never expected to get. Indeed, a phone call from Tony Blair was the last thing he expected as he settled down to his corn-flakes on the morning of 3 May 1997 . . .

'I am not aspiring to high office. Therefore I can preserve a degree of candour that perhaps cannot be retained by others. I make that point in a friendly and amicable fashion, but I can stand up and speak my mind in this place without fear or favour.'

Hansard, *21 January 1987*

'You will be a Minister in my next Government.'

Labour leader John Smith to Tony Banks, June 1993

'I realise at this late stage of the parliamentary year that my chances of legislative success are even less than my chances of entering the Kingdom of Heaven – or indeed the Shadow Cabinet, although I am assured by my more ambitious colleagues that the two are one and the same place.'

On the introduction of his Pet Animal Welfare Bill, 18 October 1995

'Is the Pope Catholic? I thought that would stand me in very good stead with Cherie and the friends of the Brompton Oratory.'

What Banks says he replied to the Prime Minister when he accepted his ministerial appointment

'I was totally and utterly gobsmacked when I got The Call. I mean that. I'm not just saying it. It was a complete and utter surprise. Because I had no reason whatsoever to expect a call. Perhaps some might argue, no justification either. So when I got the call I thought it was a spoof.

Then, when I heard the very efficient voice on the switchboard at Number Ten Downing Street, I thought "Oh no, I'm going to get told off." Perhaps the lavatories were blocked or something. Could I possibly come round with me plunger. And then it turned out it was Himself, saying I'd like you to be the new Sports Minister . . . I actually said "Fuck me!". Then I said, "I don't quite know what to say," except then, of course, I managed to say "Yes." There wasn't much of a pause between me saying "I don't know what to say" and "yes". Nanoseconds. I went for it.'

Daily Telegraph, *19 September 1997*

★

'I'm completely gobsmacked. It's a bit like going to heaven without having to die first.'

On his elevation to Minister for Sport, quoted in the Mail on Sunday, *5 April 1998*

★

'I would like you to do it because you could bring a bit of fizz and spark to it.'

Banks on what Tony Blair said to him when offering him the job of Minister for Sport, The Times, *5 May 1997*

★

'To get in there and liven it up. I was thinking after the first few days that perhaps I had exceeded my brief.'

On his task on becoming Minister for Sport

'I've not been made Foreign Secretary, where diplomatic language is essential. I shall be using the language of sport, which does get colourful from time to time.'

The Independent, *6 May 1997*

'Posh innit?'

On entering the Department of National Heritage, The Independent, *6 May 1997*

'God, this is a bit rudimentary, isn't it? It's like a prison cell. I don't think much of the trappings of office so far. Nothing in the out tray, nothing in the urgent tray, nothing in the pending tray, just the way it should be.'

On entering his ministerial office for the first time, The Independent, *6 May 1997*

'He'll be a breath of fresh air . . . I'm sure Banksy will bring a people's touch and he certainly has strong views.'

Ken Bates, Daily Telegraph, *9 May 1997*

'They've had 18 years to fuck the country up. We've had only two days. And we're not doing badly.'

In an interview with the Guardian *on his first day as a Minister, 10 May 1997*

★

'The role of a Sports Minister – after all, he is a fairly junior chap in the pecking order – is to perhaps be a catalyst, to articulate some of the problems and encourage people to come to sensible solutions. In the end I see myself as the punter in the office. I definitely see myself as a punter's minister.'

Daily Telegraph, *10 May 1997*

'As this job sits on the rankings of Westminster, it is of a humble and lowly nature. It's only one step above a gofer. But that's the view of the politicians. It isn't the view of the punters.'

Daily Telegraph, *10 May 1997*

'If I had to choose between being the Sports Minister or a Chelsea supporter, I wouldn't be the Sports Minister.'

The Independent, *17 May 1997*

'My role is to serve as the long-stop, for those who are cricketers, or as the sweeper, for those interested in soccer. I see myself as perhaps the Ruud Gullit of the Government team, although as Hon. Members will probably notice, I am considerably shorter, I am not black and I do not have dreadlocks.'

House of Commons, 27 June 1997

'Frankly, Lord MacLaurin should not have said those things about the Labour Party before the election. If one wants to hold a non-political position, to suggest that the election of a Labour Government would mean the end of civilisation as we know it is probably not a shrewd career move.'

House of Commons, 27 June 1997

'It really annoys me that these days I can get coverage for breaking wind as I walk down the road, but I cannot get coverage for the excellent international achievements of our [disabled] sportsmen and women.'

House of Commons, 27 June 1997

'Seeing someone on one leg going over a water-skiing jump is pretty formidable. It is not the sort of thing that I would do even if I had as many legs as a centipede.'

House of Commons, 27 June 1997

'I want to be spared the hordes of old buffers in blazers and caps who purport to run so many of our sports.'

House of Commons, 27 June 1997

'Sir Clifford Richard . . . is a national institution if ever there was one. I am sure that Sir Clifford will qualify for listed status fairly shortly.'

House of Commons, 23 July 1997

'I didn't expect to be a Minister and, that being so, my attitude remains one of: "Why am I here? I'm here to do something positive and useful, not just ponce around."'

Total Football, *August 1997*

'I'd rather be Minister for Sport than Secretary of State for Northern Ireland – I'll tell you that for nothing.'

Total Football, *August 1997*

'I don't like *Football's Coming Home*. That is an insult. I was in Paris listening to people sing that and *Britannia Rules the Waves*. It's pathetic. Pathetic to actually have people saying these sorts of things. It's crap.'

Total Football, *August 1997*

★

'National flags should not be carried into the stadium . . . because then sport becomes almost an extension of war. I don't think you should have the playing of national anthems before football matches. Why stir people up? I think you should glory in the sport, not the nationalism behind the sport.'

Daily Telegraph, *17 August 1997*

★

'Tony is a mate of mine but he is talking total rubbish. It is one of the stupidest suggestions he's made.'

Football agent Eric Hall, Daily Telegraph, *17 August 1997*

★

'He has not spoken to his policy advisers about this before. I think he is throwing his arguments into the fray rather than considering active legislation on the matter.'

Anonymous Department of Culture Spokesman, Daily Telegraph, *17 August 1997*

★

'Outrageous. This is a further undermining of our Britishness. It is politically correct claptrap. Singing of the National Anthem is one of our great traditions. It binds people together. This is typical of the Labour Party, bashing Britain all the time. Tony Banks may be an oddball, but he is a Government Minister and he represents Tony Blair. It is an indication of the Prime Minister's thinking.'

Lady Olga Maitland, Daily Telegraph, *17 August 1997*

★

'I am still in the job and that is sometimes as great a surprise to me as to anyone else.'

Daily Telegraph, *December 1997*

★

'For years the main complaint I heard about Tory Sports Ministers was that they didn't say anything, they were invisible men. But now whenever I say anything I'm accused of being controversial and shouting my big mouth off. Journalists, even more than politicians, want to have their cake and eat it.'

Quoted in The Observer, *8 March 1998*

★

'The idea that the only sports worth encouraging are competitive sports, you know, is bollocks. It's ideological bollocks. And I hope you ain't going to see too much ideological bollocks around here.'

The Independent, *10 May 1998*

★

'I enjoy boxing, although I don't like it when it gets gory. But seeing Prince Naseem box, seeing his movement in that, it's almost like poetry.'

The Independent, *10 May 1998*

'I detect that I am probably getting into difficult areas and I must call on my well-known fund and pool of diplomatic ability at this point.'

Evidence to the Select Committee on Culture, Media and Sport, Hansard, *14 May 1998*

'I have no intention of even thinking about being Secretary of State and I am sure that same vision is shared by the Prime Minister.'

Evidence to the Select Committee on Culture, Media and Sport, Hansard, *14 May 1998*

'There's a lot of frustration in this job. It's the frustration of not being able to get in there and say "do this do that". I'd like to be a Sports Tsar with absolute power. No one's ever going to give that to me. I do like to intervene in a more direct way because that's what I came into politics for . . . I only got involved because I wanted to do things. When you can't actually resolve a problem that you can clearly identify you get very very frustrated and in my case quite aggressive and I start saying things I subsequently feel I might have rephrased.'

Interview with Kirsty Young, Channel 5, 19 July 1998

'Well, I can assure you I didn't steal it. I was a little petrified standing out there live on telly to give an award – only to find there was nothing there. Afterwards I was annoyed. At least it wasn't my fault this time.'

After presenting a sports award to Greg Rusedski on live TV only to find that there was no award to present

'I am one of those who believe that it is ridiculous to suggest that bright kids read books and thickos do sports.'

Hansard, *27 July 1998*

★

Maybe it's Because he's a Londoner

London blood courses through Tony Banks's veins. He cut his political teeth in London politics and now stands a chance of becoming the first directly elected mayor of the nation's capital. His first years in parliament were characterised by a stoic defence of the Greater London Council and its far left policies against the onslaught of the Thatcher Government and its Bill to abolish the GLC . . .

'Totally elitist.'

On the Royal Festival Hall's champagne bar, which he closed while on the GLC

★

'The GLC is not going to be seen as some sort of South Bank equivalent of the *Belgrano* – to be destroyed merely to satisfy the power lust of the Prime Minister.'

In his maiden speech in the House of Commons

'I know what projects will be hit if this instruction is carried. I shall use what small influence I have at County Hall to ensure that we hit the constituencies of those Conservative Members who vote in favour of the instruction. There will be a certain degree of selective vindictiveness . . . I shall do my best as an individual member of the GLC to ensure that retribution is visited upon the heads of Conservative Members.'

Hansard, 12 June 1984, during a debate on the GLC's capital expenditure

★

'Here we are, about to tie up the best part of the parliamentary year on a Bill which is about as relevant to those problems as medieval discussions about the number of angels who could dance on the end of a pin.'

On the bill to abolish the GLC, Hansard, 3 December 1984

'It is a fag packet proposal written into the manifesto by the Prime Minister in a fit of great passion.'

On the bill to abolish the GLC, Hansard, 12 December 1984

'The London council I wish to see would have far greater authority than the old GLC.'

Tribune, *26 July 1990*

'I want to be the person who goes over to the first meeting of the Greater London Authority on behalf of a Labour Government and I would start with the words, "As I was saying before we were so rudely interrupted."'

Financial Times, *5 July 1991*

'Abolition [of the GLC] was an act of political malice, carried out by probably the most vindictive, dogmatic, bigoted, authoritarian Prime Minister that this country has had to suffer since the days of the Duke of Wellington – from the Iron Duke to the Iron Maiden, linked together through 150 years only by their own personal arrogance. It is not my intention to re-fight the old battles, because I cheer myself up with the old saying: "Don't get mad, get even."'

House of Commons, 21 February 1996

And what better way to get even than by becoming the people's choice as London mayor? The prospect of a contest between Tony Banks, Ken Livingstone, Steve Norris and Jeffrey Archer is one that political satirists are praying for!

'I would love to be the first directly elected mayor of London. It would be a wonderful political opportunity and I would almost certainly go for it.'

Financial Times, *5 July 1991*

'I'm definitely going to go for it.'

On the chance of being mayor of London, Mail on Sunday, 5 *April 1998*

'I have a long history of interest in this post, for example by pushing a Ten Minute Rule Bill through Parliament in 1990 which called then for a directly elected mayor of London.'

Sunday Times, *19 April 1998*

'He and I have been comrades for years.'

On Ken Livingstone after being accused of being the 'Stop Ken' candidate for mayor of London, Sunday Times, *19 April 1998*

★

'I am going for this job flat out.'

On Banks's wish to be London' s first mayor, Sunday Times, *19 April 1998*

★

'Please God, no! He is just as left-wing as Ken, slightly more loyal, but much more accident-prone.'

Anonymous Labour spin doctor on hearing of Tony Blair's apparent endorsement of Banks as mayoral candidate, Sunday Telegraph, *3 May 1998*

'I raised this in a debate in May 1990. Unlike some people, I have a track record which shows I'm no newcomer to this.'

Sunday Telegraph, *3 May 1998*

'I think that Ken is one of the greatest talents of the Labour movement that's been squandered and he's squandered it himself. I've told him this to his face. He's never punched his real weight since he's been elected to Parliament.'

On Ken Livingstone, The Guardian, *10 May 1998*

'Crawling from the wreckage of the GLC, he has survived it better than Ken Livingstone.'

The Times

'I should like to see far more planners and architects living in their creations. They usually choose to live in very low-rise and luxurious accommodation as far from the centre of London as they can get. Some of them should come back years later to see just how much damage they have done in various parts of London.'

Hansard, *24 February 1984*

'I swear that if a politician is genuinely going around London with his or her eyes open they would get as angry and homicidal as I get at times.'

London Evening Standard, *26 October 1992*

'In politics generally people say the most important slogan is: it's the economy, stupid. In London you have to adapt that: it's transport, stupid. Sort out transport and you have everyone on side.'

Sunday Times, *19 April 1998*

The Banks Career

Born	8 April 1943
Parents	Albert (diplomat) and Sally (nee Jones)
Education	St John' s Primary School, Brixton
	Archbishop Tenison' s Grammar School, Kennington
	York University
	London School of Economics
	University of London
1964	Joined Labour Party
June 1970	Contested East Grinstead in General Election
1970-77, 81-86	Elected to the GLC,
1971	Elected to Lambeth Borough Council
1973-83	Asst General Secretary, Association of Broadcasting Staff
October 1974	Contested Newcastle North
1974	Stood down from Lambeth Borough Council
1975	Appointed political adviser to Dame Judith Hart, Minister for Overseas Development
October 1977	Urges abolition of the House of Lords
May 1979	Contested Watford in General Election
November 1982	Selected for Newham North West
June 1983	Wins Newham North West with 6,918 majority
1985-86	Chairman of the GLC
1987	Elected chairman of the London Labour MPs
1990-91	Opposition spokesman on Social Security
January 1991	Voted against the Party whip on Gulf War and was sacked from the front bench
1992-93	Opposition spokesman on Transport
May 1997	Appointed Parliamentary Under Secretary of State at the Department of National Heritage

Bibliography

Dale, Iain, *As I Said to Denis – The Margaret Thatcher Book of Quotations*, Robson, 1997

Dod's Parliamentary Companion 1998

Knight, Greg, *Parliamentary Sauce*, Robson, 1993

Roth, Andrew, *Parliamentary Profiles*

Total Football magazine